A FIGHTING
SPIRIT

PAUL BURNS

A FIGHTING SPIRIT

The inspiring story of a soldier who survived the loss
of his comrades, faced adversity and overcame it all

harper
true

HarperTrue
HarperCollins*Publishers*
77–85 Fulham Palace Road,
Hammersmith, London W6 8JB

www.harpercollins.co.uk

First published by HarperTrue 2010

1 3 5 7 9 10 8 6 4 2

A catalogue record of this book is
available from the British Library

ISBN 978-0-00-735437-5

Printed and bound in Great Britain by
Clays Ltd, St Ives plc

Mixed Sources
Product group from well-managed
forests and other controlled sources
www.fsc.org Cert no. SW-COC-001806
© 1996 Forest Stewardship Council

FSC is a non-profit international organisation established to promote the
responsible management of the world's forests. Products carrying the FSC
label are independently certified to assure consumers that they come
from forests that are managed to meet the social, economic and
ecological needs of present and future generations.

Find out more about HarperCollins and the environment at
www.harpercollins.co.uk/green

Contents

	Foreword	vii
	Prologue	ix
Chapter 1	The Terror of Toton	1
Chapter 2	The Maroon Machine	14
Chapter 3	Knowledge Dispels Fear	36
Chapter 4	Warrenpoint	57
Chapter 5	Broken	68
Chapter 6	Moving On	91
Chapter 7	A Leap of Faith	110
Chapter 8	Red Devil	123
Chapter 9	The Wrong Way Round	151

A Fighting Spirit

Chapter 10   Preparing for the Race   172

Chapter 11   The Lonely Sea and the Sky   188

Chapter 12   The Southern Ocean   207

Chapter 13   Sea Change   223

Chapter 14   Not Forgotten   241

Chapter 15   The Silver Screen   256

              Dedication   273
              Acknowledgements   275

Foreword

This an extraordinary and moving story of courage and fortitude: Paul Burns, as a young soldier in the Parachute Regiment, was grievously wounded in the IRA bomb attack at Warrenpoint in Northern Ireland in 1979. He refused to let the loss of one leg and severe damage to his other foot rule his life, and went on to do so many things that might daunt fully able-bodied people: freefall parachuting, sub-aqua, motorbiking, skiing, and round-the-world sailing as a member of a disabled crew.

Paul Burns's life is a triumph of the human spirit over adversity, and a shining example to us all, able-bodied or not. It is typical of him that he has given so much to others who have lost limbs – not least by his tremendous support to the British Limbless Ex-Service Men's Association (BLESMA).

General Sir Mike Jackson

Prologue

Northern Ireland, 27 August 1979

Even the most extraordinary days start out ordinary. Today is no exception.

It's hot. Our uniforms are stifling. The air in the back of the truck in which we're travelling is heavy with exhaust fumes. I'm sitting at the back, my red beret perched firmly on my head, trying to get a few lungfuls of fresh air.

Elsewhere in the lorry I can hear my mates chatting. It's just the usual army banter. They're saying nothing of any great importance. Why would they? They don't real-ize what is about to happen. None of us does.

There are only eight of us in the truck. There might have been more, but we're laden down with boxes of ammo. Sometimes you have to be grateful for small mercies. If there had been more of us, the carnage that lies ahead would have been all the greater.

I look out of the vehicle and smile to myself. I'm just a young man, a kid from the Midlands, but already I'm seeing the world. Having an adventure. Doing what I've wanted to do ever since I was a child. And it's picturesque here. Breathtaking. The kind of place that tourists come to from far and wide to take the air and recharge their batteries. A famous beauty spot. But it's about to become famous for a very different reason.

On the left-hand side of the truck is a stretch of water, a wide estuary that separates Northern Ireland from the Republic. And, on the other side of the water, thick forest coming down to the shore. It's impossible for any of us to know what dangers those trees are hiding. Why would we even think about it? They are far away, and in any case we are members of the Parachute Regiment. We've passed one of the most rigorous selection procedures in the British Army. We are young and fit, well prepared and confident. Why should we fear what may be lurking in the woods?

The lorry trundles on. The lads continue to chat.

I continue to look out of the lorry, killing time till we reach our destination, little knowing that, for so many of my friends, time is coming to an end.

The worst horrors come without warning. The most brutal shocks are those for which you are the least prepared. And although, deep down, I know what the reality of conflict is, nothing could have prepared me for what is about to happen.

We drive past a trailer parked in a lay-by and filled with bales of hay. I do not notice it because there's nothing to notice. It's an ordinary scene. An innocent one.

And I do not hear the bang, nor the screams that follow. I do not smell the stench of burning flesh, or witness the confusion. All I know is darkness.

It's as though a curtain has been drawn. A curtain that signals the end of my old life, and the beginning of a new one, though what this new life will be like, nobody can say.

It is a darkness that means the lights of many lives have been extinguished. And that my own world can never be the same again.

Chapter One

The Terror of Toton

It was a quiet, sunny day in the early part of the 1960s when my mum received the phone call.

'Joan speaking,' she said.

It was a neighbour, Marjorie, who lived next to our comfortable house in Toton, a suburb of Nottingham.

'Er, Joan,' she said. 'Don't panic or anything. Just nip upstairs and quietly go into the back bedroom.'

'Why? What's wrong?'

'Just be quick, eh?'

So my mum put down the phone, went upstairs and opened the door to one of the bedrooms. And there she saw me. Somehow I had managed to open the window, climb into the frame, then hold onto the window itself and swing outside. I was rocking to and fro with a big smile on my face. The only problem was that I was 3 years old, and my makeshift playground was twenty feet up in the air with nothing to break my fall. Quite how Mum managed to hold it together enough to gather me in her arms and pull me back inside to safety, I don't know. But I guess, with antics like that, it's no surprise that my family started to call me the Terror of Toton.

That wasn't the only time I gave my mum cause to catch her breath. Far from it, if the stories I've heard about my earliest years are true. Our house was in a cul-de-sac about 100 metres from the busy A52. This major road linked the north Midlands with the east of England and, even in those days, it was full of lorries and other fast-moving traffic. Not the ideal place for a toddler to go walkabout, but that's just what I did, not long after the window incident. The Terror of Toton was found wandering across this road on the back of his treasured hobbyhorse, oblivious to the danger he was in.

Perhaps it's a bit too much to say that as a toddler I was a free spirit. Perhaps all toddlers are free spirits, and in many ways I was no different from a lot of children. As for so many little boys, my Action Man and soldiers were always my favourite toys. And I certainly remember being taken to a playgroup in a big Victorian building and spending the whole time sitting by the exit, waiting to be collected, while all the other kids happily played nursery games. I hated being cooped up inside – I just wanted to be out in the fresh air, left to my own devices. No doubt my tendency to swing from first-floor windows or venture alone across busy main roads was a source of some anxiety for my mum and dad, but I sometimes wonder if I've changed so much since those very early years.

Ours was a large family. When I was born, on 25 March 1961, my oldest brother John was already 18, my oldest sister Jill 16, and my youngest sister Rosalind was 8. John and Jill were more like an uncle and an aunt than a brother and sister, and I probably couldn't help but be inspired by them in some way. Jill became a midwife and John a policeman – both professions in which they served the community, just as I would aim to do when the time came for me to make my own choice of career.

My dad, Matt, worked for the TV company Rediffusion as an area manager and general troubleshooter. It was a good job and it meant we lived comfortably in a large, four-bedroomed house, had a nice car, and my older brother and sisters went away to private schools. But in 1965, just as my earliest memories start to take shape, disaster hit our happy, well-to-do family. Dad suffered a massive heart attack and stroke. He died, leaving Mum widowed with a 4-year-old boy and a 12-year-old girl to look after. So I barely remember my father, and those memories I do have come more from creased old black and white photographs and from what other people have told me about him than anything else.

What I do know is that my father's death inevitably made life very difficult for Mum. Dad was eleven years older than her, and they'd married when she was 21. All her adult life he'd been there to look after her. Now she was on her own, with no real income and two kids to care for. She sold the house and we moved into a smaller one in another part of Nottingham. Mum took a part-time job at

Rediffusion. She did the best she could, and in the circumstances she coped remarkably, but from that point on
money was always tight.

As for me, I became an independent little thing and
even as a small boy I remember feeling that I was the man
of the house, with all the duties and responsibilities that
came with it. I wasn't the type of kid to talk about the
sadness I felt, but although our family was large and
close-knit, I was constantly aware of the hole in my life
left by the death of my father. Some holes can never be
filled, and I have always carried with me a sense of that
early loss. I probably always will. And yet, even as a child,
I knew there was no point complaining about these things.
All you can do is play the hand you're dealt and get on
with your life as best you can. It was an early lesson, but
it would prove to be one of the most important I ever
learned.

I went to school at the local comprehensive. I suffer
from dyslexia, but back then I doubt they even knew what
dyslexia was – I think they just assumed I was a bit thick
when it came to letters and numbers. I was a fairly enthusiastic student, though, despite all the extra lessons I had
to take. I liked school, and I liked learning. But it was
outside the walls of the classroom that my heart really
lay.

At the end of our cul-de-sac in Toton there was an
army training camp – Chilwell Depot, which is still used
today as a mobilization centre for the Territorials before
they go off to Afghanistan. Back then it was separated

from the road by a simple chain-link fence. One of my earliest memories is of wandering to the end of the road and pressing my face up against the fence to catch a glimpse of the soldiers moving about inside. I was trans-fixed by the sight of their vehicles, and by the olive drab of their uniforms, which matched the clothes my Action Man wore. If I was lucky, I might spot one of them carry-ing a weapon. And, like any other boy, I was addicted to the war movies and cowboy films that were so popular at the end of the 1960s and the beginning of the 1970s. Throughout my early childhood the British Army held a fascination for me. So it was that, the very moment I was old enough to become part of the Army Cadet Force, at the age of 11, I joined up.

A bit like the Boy Scouts, the Army Cadet Force is a youth group where young lads are given a bit of struc-ture, discipline and the chance to have quite a lot of fun. I was issued with my very own olive-drab uniform – which I always made sure was immaculate – and once a week I would attend a drill night, and occasionally we would go away on camps. The Cadet Force was tailor-made for me. Most of the adults who ran it were ex-Army, and they taught us all the things I'd been longing to know: about guns and fieldcraft; about first aid and how to use a map and compass; about signals skills and other kinds of mili-tary know-how. As a small boy, my nose pressed against the fence of the training camp in Toton, I had wondered what it might be like to be a soldier; now I was being given the opportunity to act it all out.

The Army Cadet Force was a constructive influence in my life. It was good fun and got me out of the house, of course; but it also gave me something to work for and something positive to think about. I particularly enjoyed the camps we went on. There are several of these camps dotted around the country, where a couple of hundred cadets would descend for a few days. Because all of them actively wanted to be there, and most of them tried hard to be the best at whatever they were doing, there was always a real buzz about these places. Back then, the cadet camps were made up of old wooden huts that looked like something from the Second World War. These huts contained little more than a small pot-bellied stove in the middle, with beds arranged along either side. Basic stuff, but I loved it because it gave me the opportunity to do the one thing that I enjoyed above all others, and that was being out of doors. It was thrilling to use a map and compass to move stealthily through the woods, creeping up on other people without being heard, and to build shelters what seemed like miles from civilization. I loved being close to nature, out in the wild, learning the basic field-craft skills that would – I imagined – allow me to survive out of doors on my own.

And, like any young boy would, I enjoyed learning how to handle a gun. We would go to proper rifle ranges, ones that real, grown-up soldiers used. It was all very exciting, even though the weapons we were given to practise on were rather old bolt-action rifles that looked like relics from the First World War. They fired reasonably large rounds, though – .303s – and for a young lad the kickback from a weapon like that was quite severe. But that didn't matter to me. I was just thrilled to be taught how to fire a gun, just like the soldiers in the war movies. And sometimes, when we were away on camp, we were given the chance to drive tanks. Imagine it – barely a teenager and driving a tank. No wonder I loved the Army Cadet Force, and no wonder I thrived there. My boots were always highly polished, my uniform perfectly ironed and ready for inspection on drill nights. It instilled in me a lot of pride, self-discipline and self-reliance, and these are qualities that I hope have never left me. Being a cadet also bolstered my enthusiasm for all things military, and I became so obsessed with Airfix models that the ceiling of my bedroom started to resemble the Battle of Britain. And it meant that even when he was very young, the Terror of Toton had his sights firmly set on a career in the British Army.

The Parachute Regiment was born on 22 June 1940, but the British Army was late to the party in terms of military parachutists. As early as 1927 the Italians were developing a military parachuting unit; in 1936 the Soviet Army countered an Afghan invasion of Tajikistan using airborne soldiers; and, in the early stages of the Second World War, Germany had launched devastatingly successful assaults on the Netherlands and Belgium using glider and parachute troops. Hitler's airborne units were also crucial to the Blitzkrieg that led to the fall of France in 1940 and it was this that persuaded our Prime Minister, Winston Churchill, that Britain needed its own airborne division. In a memorandum to the Joint Chiefs of Staff, he called for a 'corps of at least five thousand parachute troops, suitably organised and equipped' as part of his plan for 'a vigorous, enterprising and ceaseless offensive against the whole German occupied coastline'.

Not everybody thought Churchill was right. As a report by the Air Staff put it:

> We are beginning to incline to the view that dropping troops from the air by parachute is a clumsy and obsolescent method and that there are far more important possibilities in gliders. The Germans made excellent use of their parachute troops in the Low Countries by exploiting surprise, and by virtue of the fact that they had practically no opposition. But it seems to us at least possible that this may be the last time that parachute troops are used on a serious scale in major operations.

They were overruled. A Parachute Training School was set up at Ringway airfield, near Manchester, and the men of No. 2 Commando – one of fifteen Commando units that Churchill had tasked to 'develop a reign of terror down the enemy coast' – were selected to train with parachutes.

No. 2 Commando became the 11th Special Air Battalion, before mutating into the Parachute Regiment in 1942.

The Paras' first operation took place in February 1941, when they were dropped into Italy and destroyed the Tragino Aqueduct in Apulia. Nearer home, in early 1942 they pulled off a daring raid during which they removed vital components from a German radar installation on the Normandy coast. They were also deployed in North Africa, where the Germans dubbed them 'Die Roten Teufeln' – the 'Red Devils' – on account of their maroon berets. Churchill's conviction that the British Army needed a parachute regiment was more than justified, and after the Second World War the Paras would go on to see active service in, among other places, the Far East, Aden, Cyprus, and, when I was still a teenager, Northern Ireland. They had a reputation for being some of the toughest, most fearless, most respected soldiers in the British Army.

I was about 14 when the Parachute Regiment came to Nottingham, and I knew none of this. I only knew I loved soldiers and soldiering, which was why I went to a big Army show in the Old Market Square, a large, old-fashioned space in the centre of the city. It was here that the Parachute Regiment Display Team had set up shop. Of course, I was interested in all aspects of the Army, but it was these soldiers who immediately caught my eye. There was something about them, something that set them apart from all the others. Perhaps it was their air of confidence, or perhaps it was just the way they dressed. They wore parachute smocks, for a start, and had a different sort of camouflage uniform. And, of course, they wore the famous red beret.

The Paras had erected a tower in the middle of the square. It must have been about fifty feet high – although to me at that age it no doubt looked twice that – and we were allowed to perform simulated parachute jumps from the top of it. It was by far the most exciting thing I'd ever done. The tower, I now know, was a fan descender. Kitted out in a parachute harness, you attached yourself to a cable. Down below, at the other end of this cable, was a fan that slowed your descent to a speed similar to that of a real parachute jump – about twenty feet per second. I was awed by the experience.

Long before that day I knew that I wanted to join the Army, and I knew that I wanted to be a soldier – the best solder I could possibly be – rather than a military mechanic or an engineer. And when I saw the Red Berets in the Old Market Square that day, I realized that I wanted to be in the Parachute Regiment. Whenever I mentioned it to anyone, they would suck their teeth and warn me how hard it was to get in, and how gruelling the training would be if I was accepted. The Parachute Regiment was only for the best of the best. That only made me want to join it all the more.

Still, it seemed a big step from being a teenage Army cadet to signing up with my revered Paras. But when I started what was to be my last year at school, an Army recruiting officer came to talk to us. His job was to try to persuade classrooms full of teenage kids that joining up was a great way to see the world and get a bit of excitement. I don't know what effect his words had on my peers, but as far as I was concerned, he was preaching to the converted. I couldn't quite believe it could all be that easy – I didn't even have to go and ask anyone about joining the Army. They had come to me! I told the officer that I wanted to join the Parachute Regiment. No teeth-sucking from him. No words of discouragement. He just gave me a big smile and a piece of paper to sign.

Soon afterwards the Army invited me to go on an assessment course. This lasted about a week and was a bit like *The Krypton Factor* – a series of mental, aptitude and physical tests – but I passed easily enough and was given the green light to join the Army as a junior soldier when I left school. I was over the moon. I'd always wanted to be a soldier, and now I didn't have to worry about what I was going to do when my schooling was over. I certainly had no worries that I was embarking upon a dangerous career. Why would I? I was only 16, and quite unaware of the realities of those conflicts that had filled the public consciousness as I was growing up, like the Vietnam War or the Troubles in Northern Ireland. I was embarking upon an adventure, and looking forward to it.

And so I joined up, along with a friend from the Army Cadet Force called Ralph – a big guy with a black belt in judo. Filled with excitement, we travelled down to Aldershot to begin our training with 30 Platoon, Junior

Parachute Company, at Browning Barracks. It felt like a big step, flying the nest and joining the college-like atmosphere at Aldershot. We still had the benefit of school holidays, but now we actually earned a wage. It was a pittance really – enough to buy boot polish and toothpaste, just about – but all the same it felt good to have money in your pocket.

The emphasis at Aldershot was on sport and fitness with lots of outside activities, including trips to go canoeing, climbing and potholing all round the country. I remember camping out in the Devil's Punch Bowl in Surrey in a foot of snow, which was just the sort of thing I loved. It wasn't for everyone, though. Ralph dropped out after about six weeks, having decided that the disciplined environment wasn't for him. He wasn't the only one. A lot of people left, for a variety of reasons, but I stuck it out.

Whenever I went back home to Nottingham, I felt that my eyes had been opened to a whole new way of life. A lot of the guys I had grown up with had simply moved from school into a dead-end job in the local pit or in some dreary factory. The biggest thing they had to talk about was that they were going out with a new girl, or had started drinking in a different pub. When they asked me what I'd been doing, I was able to say that I'd been potholing, or shooting, or climbing. I felt my life was fuller as a result of being a junior soldier, and it spurred me on. I may have been young, but I knew how I wanted things to pan out.

I wanted to progress to the full-blown Parachute Regiment. To don the red beret.

Chapter Two

The Maroon Machine

At the age of 17 I moved on from the junior Paras and into 448 Platoon, Recruit Company, part of the training and assessment wing of the Parachute Regiment.

My time in Recruit Company would last six months, and right from day one I knew that I was embarking upon just about the most difficult training and selection regime that the regular British Army has to offer. The Parachute Regiment attracts all manner of men, so as well as others from all over the UK, I rubbed shoulders with Rhodesians and New Zealanders and even an Australian submariner who had decided he wanted a change of scene. New recruits are known as 'Crows', 'Joe Crow' being the personification of the new recruit. The youngsters who had come together in the Parachute Regiment Depot at Browning Barracks were there with the express intention of making the transition from a Crow to a Tom.

We were a pretty motley crew, even after those few guys who realized they'd made a big mistake had exercised their 'discharge by right', which meant they were allowed to leave within the first eight weeks on payment of a £100 fee. For a lot of young lads, it is their first time away from home. Going from a nice, cosy house where your mum makes your bed to having your hair shaved off and being under the watchful eye of one of Recruit Company's training corporals – some of the regiment's most respected and fearsome members – can be a bit of a shock to the system. No wonder that a fair few decide rather quickly that the Army is not for them.

But I was used to it, from my time as a junior soldier. In fact those of us who had already spent time at Aldershot were excused the first couple of weeks of training, during which new recruits were issued uniforms and taught the basics of Army life. The same went for my closest friends, two lads who had joined up as junior soldiers at the same time as me, and were now in the same section of Recruit Company. Their names were Ian Wood and Jeff Jones – Woody and Jonesy – and I also made friends with guys from other sections, like Taff Davies, Taff Elliott, and Graham Eve. Woody, Jonesy and I hit it off the moment we met. Like the rest of our intake, they were straightforward, friendly guys. Woody was a cheeky little chap, always smiling, always happy. The kind of lad who's always fun to have around. Jonesy was the tallest guy in the Company. I was the second tallest, so when we were on parade we were always next to each other. The three of us were billeted together in the juniors, and thick as thieves in Recruit Company. There was an amazing camaraderie among us, I suppose because we all wanted the same thing – we were driven, professional and hungry to succeed, even though most of us were very young.

We were taught regimental history – about Churchill and the Parachute Regiment's exploits during the Second World War and afterwards. It was important stuff, not because the training corporals wanted to turn out an intake of historians, but because they wanted to hammer home the Paras' belief in their own excellence. I remember being taught the words of Field Marshal Montgomery:

> What manner of men are these who wear the maroon beret?
>
> They are, first, all volunteers, and are toughened by hard physical training. As a result, they have that infectious optimism and that offensive eagerness which come from physical well-being.
>
> They have jumped from the air and, by doing so, have conquered fear.
>
> Their duty lies in the van of battle: they are proud of their honour, and have never failed in any task.
>
> They have the highest standards in all things, whether it be skill in battle or smartness in execution of all peacetime duties.

They have shown themselves to be as tenacious
and determined in defence as they are courageous
in attack.

They are, in fact, men apart.

Every man an emperor.

It was stirring stuff, and although it would be true to say
that during the rigours of Recruit Company we didn't feel
entirely emperor-like, it was certainly inspiring to know
that if we worked hard enough we could become part of
this elite band.

Recruit Company's aim was twofold: to train the
wannabe Paras and get their skills and fitness up to
scratch; and to weed out those recruits who weren't fully
suited to joining the regiment. As well as the intense
training, we had tests at regular intervals. Anyone who
failed to meet the grade at any of these levels would be
'back-squadded', or made to retake that part of the course
with the group who had joined after them. It happened to
a lot of the guys, who found themselves unable to
progress, either through lack of fitness or through injury.
As the six months wore on, our numbers began to dwin-
dle. I worked hard, but I also had my fair share of luck
because the training became increasingly physical and
increasingly brutal. We were put through our paces like
never before, but we also underwent mental challenges
such as sleep deprivation in an attempt to weed out those
recruits who weren't mentally tough enough to progress.
We were sent on forced marches – mile after mile with full

kit and personal weapons, with the promise of a truck waiting over the next hill that never seemed to be there. It sounds harsh, but it was necessary. As a soldier, you never know what difficulties you're going to find yourself up against. (This is even more true now than it was in the days when I joined up. In Afghanistan, our young soldiers have to live in one of the harshest environments in the world, and each time they step outside they know they are going to be shot at.) The Parachute Regiment has a reputation for being able to cope with any situation, of being harder than any other regiment. Our training was specially designed to make sure we lived up to that reputation.

The days seemed to fly by. We were up at 0700 hours, and stood down at 2000. If you weren't training during that time, you were studying; if you weren't studying you were trying to get some 'scoff' down your throat in a desperate attempt to put back some of the calories you'd lost during your fitness exercises. And when the lights went out, you slept the sleep of the dead.

We were beasted. Not bullied – at no point during my career in the British Army do I remember anything remotely resembling bullying. Beasting is different. It's a way of keeping you on your toes, of making sure that you're at the peak of physical fitness. A beasting could happen any time. You might be grabbing a rare moment of relaxation in the block after a hard day's wading through rivers with full pack and rifle, when you'd hear a scream from outside your room.

'*Corridor!*'

Instantly you had to present yourself in the corridor, where an instructor would have that look on his face that you just *knew* meant something unpleasant was around the corner.

'*Position!*'

This meant you had to lean back against the wall in a sitting position with your arms out straight in front of you, but there was nothing to support your legs. Your knees would tremble; the muscles in your legs would burn. And you had to maintain that position for as long as you were told. Why? No reason, other than to make sure you were up to it. When you were up for inspection, you had to have yourself and your locker absolutely spotless, your boots gleaming, the floor of the barrack block polished to perfection. No matter how flawless you made things, you could bet that your locker would be emptied out all over the floor, or your boots flung out of the window, and you'd have to start all over again. Our days became a constant flurry of runs – over assault courses or through water up to your waist – and press-ups. The fitter you got, the faster and longer you were expected to exercise. Make the slightest mistake in a drill and the shout would go up: 'Down and give me ten!'

If you were the right kind of person for the Paras, these beastings would make you more determined that they weren't going to break you. If you were the wrong kind of person, you'd up and leave. That was the whole point.

It was the hardest thing I've ever done. Lots of guys left, but the more that fell by the wayside, the more confidence it gave those of us who remained. It felt good to be the ones who were left. Of the seventy-odd members of our Recruit Company who started out, only about twenty made it through, including myself, Woody and Jonesy. And as our training progressed, the bond between the successful recruits grew strong. We lived together in four-man rooms, and that four-man unit was the basis of everything we did. The tougher things became, the more the connection between us developed. We were all going through the same thing, so we understood how our mates were feeling. As we were pushed really hard in our training, we played equally hard in what little free time we had. A lot of drinking went on − Aldershot became a pretty entertaining place on a Friday night when all the soldiers came out to play − but our downtime was in many ways as important as our training time, because it all helped to strengthen the bond between us.

Looking back, I can see why this was an essential part of the training process. In operational situations, it would be crucial that we were able to communicate effectively with each other, sometimes without speaking. Perhaps we would be on patrol in the jungle, creeping silently through the bush and having to communicate with just a glance or a nod of the head. Or perhaps we would be soldiering in a more urban environment, and it was no secret during Recruit Company that the successful candidates would most likely end up doing a stint in Northern Ireland.

There it was vital that each member of a four-man unit constantly watched his mates' backs, and that everyone had an instinctive understanding of when something was wrong and an innate trust that the others would do whatever was necessary to see him right. All this was built up by the training and selection process – by living together, training together, sharing the same room, going to the mess, and drinking together. Your relationship with your mates became like a relationship with a girl – you knew in your gut when something wasn't right just by looking at them and reading the look on their face. In the Army you fight for Queen and Country, but in reality you're fighting for your mates, for the guys standing next to you in the battlefield. Effective soldiers are the ones who want to do this.

So, as people left Recruit Company, through injury, or after deciding this wasn't the life for them, or simply being unable to take the pace, those of us who remained grew closer. But we all knew we still had another hurdle to cross before the end of our training was in sight. This was Pegasus Company, or P Company – the pre-parachute selection course. If you pass P Company, you've qualified for your red beret. Then you can go on to do your parachute training and get your wings.

Nowadays P Company takes place at the Infantry Training Battalion in Catterick, North Yorkshire, but back then it was in Aldershot. It exists not only for the Paras, but for any soldier or officer who wishes to serve with the airborne forces. And although this is a pre-parachute selection course, it has nothing to do with parachuting. Nobody was interested in our head for heights or the strength of our ankles for landing. It wasn't even much to do with military ability – the P Company team aren't concerned with drill or fieldcraft. Instead, the course exists to assess the recruits' endurance, persistence and courage under extreme stress, to see whether they are made of the right stuff to serve with the airborne forces. It was everything we'd been building up to.

P Company consists of eight tests taken over five consecutive days. For seven of these tests you are given a score, while one of them is a matter of a straight pass or fail. At the end of the week, if you've got enough points, you're through. The trouble is, only the instructors know what the pass mark is. P Company one of the hardest recruitment tests in the British Army, and not for the faint-hearted.

Day one starts off with a steeplechase. For us this involved jumping off scaffolding poles into stinking water which we had to wade through before taking one of only two slippery, awkward exit points on the other side. If you don't get to the water quickly enough, you have to wait your turn while the other recruits make their exit, before continuing the 1.3-kilometre obstacle course. And then, when you've finished, you have to do it again. The steeplechase is against the clock – you're aiming to complete it in under nineteen minutes. For every thirty seconds you go over that, you lose a point. It's a killer.

When you've finished the steeplechase, there's barely any time to rest. Next up is the log race, for which we were divided into teams of eight. Each team had to carry a telegraph pole weighing 130 pounds over two miles of bumpy terrain, the idea being to simulate having to manoeuvre an anti-tank gun in battle. It might not sound much, but in fact this is one of the toughest challenges P Company can throw at you – the thirteen or so minutes that it takes are some of the longest of your life. The flat sections of the log race take place on loose sand, and if you've ever tried to run along a sandy beach you'll know how difficult that can be.

The afternoon of the first day sees an event known as milling. Two recruits of approximately the same size and weight are given boxing gloves, put into a ring together, and expected to slog it out for sixty seconds. That may not sound like a long time, but trust me: a minute of milling passes very slowly indeed. This isn't a test of your boxing skills, because you have points deducted for blocking or dodging a punch. It's a test of your ability to demonstrate controlled aggression, and to endure the aggression of the other guy. There's no winner or loser in a milling competition, and there's no complaining or backing out either. You either perform or you don't. And if you don't perform, you have to go again. Today the recruits wear mouth guards and head protectors, but when I went through P Company all we had was our gloves.

After the milling, the Crows get a weekend of rest – a weekend during which we were advised to do nothing but eat and sleep, because we had a hell of a time ahead of us over the next few days.

Monday morning means the ten-mile tab, or march. We all had to carry a thirty-pound Bergen (not including water), ammunition and individual weapon, and to pass we had to complete the march in under an hour and three-quarters. It sounds tough – it *is* tough – but it's important. When a soldier is parachuted in on an operation, his objective could easily be ten miles from the drop zone, or DZ. And it would be marching like this that would get 2 Para into Goose Green during the Falklands War just a few years later. When you're in enemy territory and your only mode of transport is your boots, you need to have the endurance to keep going.

Again, no time to rest, because next up was the trainasium. This is a particularly challenging test – a mid-air assault course the purpose of which is to test the recruits' confidence and ability to overcome fear. Narrow planks that you could easily walk along if they were a couple of feet off the ground become a different prospect when you're twenty metres up in the air. And jumping wide gaps that look bigger than they really are because one side is slightly lower than the other takes a lot of psychological strength when you're that high up. You're being tested here on your ability to control fear, and on your swift reaction to an order. When an instructor shouts 'Go!', you have to jump that gap, even though every cell in your body is screaming at you not to. The trainasium presents you with challenges that anyone with any sense would just walk away from, and it's this event which is a straight pass or fail. Pass and you move on to the next stage; fail and you're packing up your kit and heading home. I had to tell myself that so many people had done it before me but *I* was going to do it better. That is the mindset that six months of Recruit Company gives you.

The next day came the stretcher race. We were divided into teams of sixteen and had to carry an 180-pound steel stretcher over a distance of five miles. No more than four people were allowed to carry the stretcher at any one time, while the others carried their rifles. The stretcher race is designed to test your capacity to evacuate a wounded colleague from the battlefield, but more than that it is a fearsome test of your team-working abilities. Swapping positions, swapping weapons – all this takes coordination, communication, and, above all, the ability to work together. Winning or losing the race made no difference to your final score – the instructors judged you according to how well you presented yourself within a group.

The two-mile march, like the ten-mile march, was performed with a full pack and rifle. Time limit: eighteen minutes. And finally, the twenty-mile endurance march: full pack and rifle, and four and a half hours to complete it.

Nobody wants to fail P Company, naturally. But none of the training NCOs who have been putting the hopefuls through Recruit Company wants any of their boys to fail because it reflects badly on them. We had a chap called Rooster Barber – six foot across the shoulders and built like a brick outhouse – and he was determined that not one of his lads was going to fail. He beasted us like never before. In the days leading up to P Company he had us up before breakfast running around and jumping over benches with our rifles above our heads. Then each evening he gave us no chance to rest but blasted us with more and more fitness exercises. By the time P Company came along, we were at the peak of physical fitness. Thanks to Rooster Barber and his regular beastings, we all gave a pretty good account of ourselves in P Company and came out the other end successfully. It was a gruelling week, but all in all an amazing experience for a 17-year-old kid. At the end of it I was awarded my red beret, and that made it all worthwhile.

With the hurdle of P Company successfully negotiated, I was able to move on to parachute training at RAF Brize Norton in Oxfordshire – an enormous, sprawling airfield the size of a fair-sized town, and with many of the facilities of one too. Living accommodation, messes, recreation facilities, all surrounded by the constant thunder of VC10 and Hercules aircraft taking off and landing. It's a busy, bustling place, and although the huts along the edge of the complex where we were billeted were pretty basic, I was excited to be there after the long months of Recruit Company.

Our basic training was centred on an area of Brize Norton called No. 1 Parachute Training School. This was just a tiny part of an airfield, consisting of an aircraft hangar for ground-school training, and an administrative office block. On a separate part of the airfield was an area set aside for the outdoor training equipment. The two components of this were the Tower, which resembled an enormous column of scaffolding with a crane arm on the top, from which we could get used to falling through the air, and the Exit Trainer – or 'knacker-cracker' as it was affectionately known – from which we could practise the crucial moment when you exit the aircraft.

Parachute training is run by the RAF, which meant we were suddenly in an entirely different environment. In the Army you find yourself doubling up – or running – everywhere. At Brize Norton I was astonished to find coaches laid on to take us to the hangars. I remember turning to Woody and saying, 'It's a trick. They're going to drive us ten miles out into the countryside and make us run back.'

Woody nodded ruefully. He was wise to the Army's ways as well.

But it wasn't a trick. No. 1 Parachute Training School isn't like the Army. Its motto is 'Knowledge Dispels Fear'. We weren't here to be beasted, we were here to learn the basics of parachuting. I didn't know at the time how much this would change my life.

To start with, we found ourselves in the large aircraft hangar where we were to undergo ground-school training. The goal is to learn how to put your parachute on, then how to land properly – with your feet and knees together and your elbows in so that you can perform a special parachute roll when you hit the ground. We practised in that hangar ad nauseam, learning the movements required for exit, flight and landing, repeating them over and over so that they became second nature. They had to be, because when it comes to a real parachute jump, you're on your own. The time to make mistakes is in the hangar, not in the air. As time passed we progressed from a fake Hercules fuselage suspended a couple of feet above the crash mats to a piece of apparatus called the Fan. This was much like the machine I had jumped from back in Nottingham, but that seemed a long time ago now. The Fan, or a version of it, had originally been an attraction at a French funfair. When an English parachutist saw it, he brought the idea back to No. 1 Parachute Training School. It certainly gives you a taste of what it's like to fall through the air.

We were taught how to check our parachute for problems, and what to do if it had failed to balloon properly. Before my day nobody bothered to teach you what to do if your parachute failed, because there was nothing you could do about it anyway. But in 1955 the reserve chute arrived and if things went pear-shaped, you had options. We listened especially carefully to that part of our lessons.

For the second week of our training we moved out of our hangar and over to the Tower, that huge, steel-framed apparatus on the edge of the airfield. Here we practised leaping into nothingness while attached to a harness and wire; the instructors suspended us in mid-air so that we could perform our flight drills, before lowering us to the ground to perfect our landings. And then it was the 'knacker-cracker', which was supposed to simulate the moment of exiting the aircraft but didn't really come close.

Once we'd mastered the basics, the next stage was to perform some practice jumps, not out of an airplane, but from an enormous gas-filled balloon – an elderly thing that looked like the little brother of the *Hindenburg*. Operated by means of a winch, it had a little basket underneath, large enough for four of us plus the jump instructor. It slowly creaked up to a height of 800 feet, and once you're up there, the only way is down. It took some courage to step out of that basket for the first time, even though for those early jumps we were using static-line parachutes. These are chutes which are attached to the aircraft – or in this case the balloon – by a webbing line. As you fall away, the line automatically opens the parachute, so you don't have to do it yourself.

That first jump is vivid in my mind, even now. The eerie silence all around as I waited for the moment to arrive. No engine noise up here, no rush of wind. Just stillness, so high above the earth, and dry fear as the balloon, which has been rising steadily from the safety of the earth, comes to a halt. I looked down from the basket, knowing there was only one way I could get back down.

Suddenly I felt rather as if I was back on the trainasium again, waiting for the instruction to jump and knowing that, when it came, I would have no option but to follow the order.

I stood in the door, my arms across the reserve parachute on my chest, and on the command '*Go!*' stepped from the cage. There was a churning sensation as I fell into empty space, leaving my stomach far behind. And in the split second before my parachute automatically engaged, questions started echoing through my mind. *Is my chute going to open? Has it been packed properly? Do I trust the person who rigged it? Do I trust that I'm going to come out of this alive?* Every parachutist puts his faith in the skill of the person who rigged his gear, because every parachutist puts his life in their hands.

You drop like a stone from the balloon. In many ways it is scarier than jumping from an aircraft because there's no slipstream to hold you up. It's impossible not to be scared when you do your first jump, but it's exhilarating too. A moment that stays with you.

And then it's time for your first aircraft jump – a 'clean fatigue' jump, which means that it is performed without any extra equipment such as your Bergen or your rifle. I'll never forget the first time I shuffled into a crowded Hercules, one of about fifty parachutists being herded like sheep into a particularly unpleasant sheep pen. The Hercules is a transport aircraft, so it's entirely free of creature comforts – a bit like being ferried around in a freight train. The seats, such as they are, are little more than webbing straps attached to a metal frame, so that the interior weighs as little as possible. The aircraft's cavernous belly reeks of fuel. And as the plane makes its ascent, the constant, noisy drone seems to fill your head. It's almost impossible to speak over the sound of the engines, and on that first jump no one feels very talkative anyway. We were packed in like nervous sardines, one line of men facing another and squeezed so tightly that our knees were touching. I remember anxiously watching up ahead the red light that would turn to green when the time came to hurl ourselves into the air. Half of me couldn't wait for that moment to come; half of me wished it never would.

When fifty people jump out of an airplane in an exercise like this, the idea is to get them all landing as close to each other as possible, rather than scattered around the countryside. To achieve this, the aircraft needs to be as low as possible above the drop zone – the higher it is, the more scope there is for the parachutists to drift – and the guys need to jump out as quickly as possible. As the noisy, fumy Hercules climbed to 1,000 feet – low enough for a quick landing, but high enough to give the trainees time to sort out any problems on the way down – we all made sure that our static lines were attached to the cable above us. And when the RAF jumpmasters gave the word, we started to approach the exits on both sides of the Hercules.

When lots of people jump, it's important that they are staggered, otherwise they can collide in mid-air and get knocked unconscious or swing through each other's lines. Worst of all is an 'air steal'. This happens when one para-chutist drifts immediately over another and the lower parachute 'steals' the air that would ordinarily be filling the upper one, causing it to collapse. If this happens, the top parachutist will go into freefall until he as at the bottom, at which point his canopy inflates and steals the air of the second parachutist. Clearly if this happens too close to the ground, it can be extremely dangerous. So the jumpmasters do what they can to ensure that the para-chutists exit in a staggered, orderly fashion. Not easy when you're all crushed up together, nervously waiting to hurl yourselves out.

I can still remember the side doors of the Hercules opening.

The noise grew even louder, a screaming, roaring rush in our ears.

Suddenly the red light turned to green.

And then the jumpmasters shouted, '*Go! Go! Go!*'

Ahead of me I saw figures simply disappearing into the air, and the line moved up very quickly. Before I knew it I was at the front, and the jumpmaster was hitting me on the shoulder. '*Go!*'

I toppled out, trying not to think of all the things that could go wrong, and the world opened up below me. I felt the familiar sensation of leaving my stomach behind, but then, almost immediately, the static line kicked in and my canopy opened. I looked up and checked that all was as it should be. Was the canopy a good, round shape? Were there any holes or tears? Everything appeared to be fine, so I allowed myself to enjoy the trip back down to earth.

When I hit the ground after that first aircraft jump – knees together, elbows in, fall to the side, just like I'd been taught – I knew I'd been bitten by the bug. Despite the unpleasantness of being squashed up in the Hercules, despite the knowledge that things can, and do, go wrong when you're jumping in a military environment, all I wanted to do was get back up in the air, to experience the adrenalin buzz all over again. I wasn't alone, as there are very few people who decide, once they've done their first jump, that it isn't for them, especially after all the months of hard work that have gone before.

All in all we did about eight jumps during our parachute training, including a night jump – enough to make us reasonably proficient. After that, we were told, there would be a refresher course every year or so, to keep our skills up. In the event, though, my next parachute drop would take place under very different circumstances.

I was not yet 18 when I received my wings at a Parachute Regiment Wings Parade. The Red Devils, the regimental parachute team, jumped in, and the regimental colonel was in attendance. It was an emotional moment, one I'd worked towards ever since the day I first became a junior soldier. I'd been imbued with the spirit of the regiment – that feeling that I was one of an elite band of soldiers. The best. I had my red beret, whereas everyone else, in the language of the Paras, was just a 'crap hat'. I was part of the Maroon Machine, no longer a Crow, but a Tom. There was a lot of friendly rivalry between regiments, but it was encouraged and it all served a purpose: to give us confidence in our ability to do our job supremely well. Bullets, I thought, now that I was a member of the Parachute Regiment, would bounce off me.

There are some people who join the Army because they crave the excitement, and it's true that there was a part of me – the part that as a boy loved war films and getting stuck in with the Army Cadets – that was looking forward to the thrill of belonging to the Parachute Regiment. After all, it's not a unit you join if you're after a cushy time. But that wasn't the only reason. The truth was that I relished the idea of service. Maybe it was because I had grown up seeing my older brother serving in the police force and my sister working as a nurse. Maybe it was just something inside me. But I was attracted to the notion that I would be protecting the country. Caring for people and helping them. I was looking forward to it.

And I had my life all planned out. I had signed up to the Army for nine years and I was going to see that through. Then I'd spend some time travelling the world – maybe I'd go to Africa or somewhere else exotic and exciting. And then, when the time came, I wanted to become a fireman, because, just like being in the Army, it combined excitement and service.

The day I won my wings and donned the red beret, I was young and full of optimism. I was looking forward to a long and successful career with the Paras.

I could never have imagined how differently things would turn out.

Chapter Three

Knowledge Dispels Fear

Now that I was a full-blown Para – to be precise, a member of 2nd Battalion, the Parachute Regiment, or 2 Para – I knew that at some point in the not-too-distant future I would be deployed to Northern Ireland. We all did – Woody, Jonesy and me. The Paras had been in the Province on and off ever since British armed forces moved in during the summer of 1969, under the umbrella of Operation Banner, which was to last until 2007, and they were preparing to return for another tour of duty. It was only a matter of time before we joined them.

First, however, we needed to undergo some pre-Northern Ireland training. In addition, the Parachute Regiment had responsibilities in parts of the world other than Northern Ireland. Once of these places was Berlin, and it was there that I was deployed in January 1979.

It's easy, in the early part of the twenty-first century, to forget the tensions that seeped through Europe during the years of the Cold War. As a young man I was more concerned with soldiering than with international politics, but I took the time to acquaint myself with the history of that scarred city before I arrived.

Berlin had been under military occupation since the end of the Second World War. The victorious Allies had carved the city into Zones of Occupation at the Yalta Conference in 1945. There were British, American and French zones in the west, and in the east, bigger than any of these, the Russian zone. The idea was that Berlin should be governed equally by the four powers, but as the Cold War grew chillier the Russians excluded themselves from that joint administration.

For about fifteen years the citizens of Berlin were able to move fairly freely between the four zones. But as time went on, the inhabitants of the Russian sector grew dissatisfied with the communist regime. Increasingly large numbers of them started to migrate from the eastern part of the city to the western. So it was that in 1961, the year I was born, the Russians started to erect a wall. The Berlin Wall, and its infamous crossing point Checkpoint Charlie, became a symbol of the wider struggle between the rival political ideologies of the West and the East. Along sections of the wall were series of crosses commemorating those citizens shot by the East German border police while trying to escape into West Berlin.

If the wall symbolized communism's stand against capitalism, the whole of West Berlin was the West's rejoinder. Entirely surrounded by communist East

Germany, it was situated more than 100 miles inside Soviet-occupied territory, a focal point for the Cold War. In 1948 the Soviets had blockaded all the roads and rail links into West Berlin in an attempt to literally starve the city, but the Allies managed to keep it going by means of a continuous airlift of supplies, and a year later the Soviets ended their blockade. Nevertheless, this situation had highlighted just how vulnerable West Berlin was. The threat from behind the Iron Curtain seemed very real indeed, and it was in no way fanciful to imagine that the Russians might make a nuclear strike against the West.

When I was sent to West Berlin, the city was crawling with soldiers. There were three Allied Infantry Brigades, which included the British Berlin Infantry Brigade, made up of three battalions, including 2 Para. Our reason, in principle, for being there was to halt the Russian hordes should the Soviet Union decide to invade Europe from the east. Of course, nobody was under any illusions about what that meant. If they did invade, we would be surrounded and vastly outnumbered. Our commanders clearly knew this too, and that was why the Berlin Infantry Brigade had been given the oldest tanks and other equipment. In truth the presence of so many Allied forces in Berlin was largely symbolic: an expression of the West's refusal to surrender the city to the Soviets.

I'll always remember arriving there on 1 January 1979, a fresh-faced Tom with my mates Woody and Jonesy. The temperatures were Arctic and the parade ground at our barracks was a mountain of snow because of the need to keep the paths around it clear. We arrived there carrying all our worldly goods, pleased to have joined the battalion, but a bit nervous too, and I'm sure we looked it. We were standing at the barrack gate when a corporal by the name of Norrie Porter approached us.

'You lot new?' he asked.

We nodded.

'Got any German money?'

Of course, none of us had, so Norrie put his hand in his pocket and pulled out a few banknotes. 'That's all I've got,' he said, and handed them round. 'Go on. Go and settle in and get yourself down to the NAAFI for a coffee and some scoff.'

It was a small act of kindness – new recruits are generally the lowest of the low within a regiment, and given all the worst jobs to do – but it was typical of the group mentality of the Paras and it made us immediately feel as though we belonged.

Berlin was an amazing place to a teenager who'd never been abroad before. We worked hard, we partied hard, and as we were serving abroad we took full advantage of the duty-free drinks in the NAAFI, as well as getting to know the bars and clubs of both the borough of Spandau, where we were stationed, and of central Berlin. One night we went to see the great Muhammad Ali perform in an exhibition fight – a bit of a disappointment really, as he graced the ring for just a three-minute bout. But we were too busy, and money was too tight, for us to really see the side of the city that had earned Berlin a reputation as a centre of hedonism. Spandau itself didn't look as if it had changed much since the war – it still had a rather old-fashioned feel about it, as if we were living in a time warp.

A couple of times we passed through Checkpoint Charlie and visited East Berlin. We were obliged to do this in units of four, wearing our No. 2 Dress – uniform reserved for those occasions when you had to look super-smart. Back then you could get four East German Ostmarks for one West German Deutschmark, which meant that even we could afford to sit in the nicest restaurants eating the best food. But the atmosphere behind the wall was bleak. Everything seemed very Spartan, quieter, poorer, and more subdued – as if the citizens of East Berlin were afraid to be seen enjoying themselves. But that didn't stop some of them trying to persuade us to take their money and buy things in the West for them that they could never get their hands on otherwise. One guy asked me to bring him over a saxophone – very difficult to buy in East Germany – which really underlined the difference between our two cultures.

One of my reasons for joining the Army was to see the world. I was certainly doing that, and my first tour in Berlin seemed to justify the choices I'd made. I was enjoying myself, proud to be a Para, and looking forward to the challenges that my career would hold. But, of course, we weren't there just to go sightseeing. In fact we were worked very hard indeed. My mates and I were deployed all around the British sector of West Berlin, guarding bridges and other points of strategic importance, ready to defend them the best we could if things should kick off. Looking back, it seems rather comical. Nobody would like the odds of a few rookie paratroopers successfully defending an attack from all sides by the massed might of the Soviet Army. Even then, it all seemed like a bit of a joke. Me and my band of newly badged Toms never seriously thought the Russians were going to invade. We were just thrilled to have got through training and excited to have finally joined the battalion.

Once a month our platoon would be on standby, which meant being stationed at the British Army HQ ready to be deployed at two minutes' notice. On other occasions we would be instructed to perform guard duty at Spandau prison. This famous jail was originally built to hold more than 100 prisoners. But after the Second World War, it played host to only seven – all of them Nazi war criminals sentenced to imprisonment after the Nuremberg Trials. By the time I arrived, six of them had been released, leaving only one: Rudolf Hess, Hitler's deputy, whom I remember seeing from a distance as he strolled round the exercise yard. The prison no longer exists. After Hess's death in 1987 it was totally destroyed to stop it becoming a Nazi shrine.

Our six months in Berlin was not solely given over to protecting the West from the supposed threat of a Russian incursion, or guarding Nazi war criminals. We still had to undergo our continuation training, because when a recruit leaves the Para depot his training is not finished: old skills need to be refreshed and new ones learned. So, one day, after we'd been in Berlin for a few weeks, the call went up: '*Inter-company fifty-mile march!*'

I turned to Jonesy. 'Are they joking?'

They weren't joking. An inter-company race. None of us had ever done a march that long before – not even during P Company – and this was to be done with personal weapon and belt-order – a solid reminder that, although we'd finished our training, life in the Parachute Regiment was no walk in the park.

There were some moments of real excitement. Gatow Airport, in south-west Berlin, was a major strategic location within the British sector. The RAF troops stationed there needed to know how to defend it should it come under attack. For its training exercises, the Parachute Regiment had to pretend to be invaders. This involved flying over in American Hueys – the iconic American chopper that you see in all the Vietnam movies – since we didn't have any aircraft big enough for troop transportation on that scale. We wore helmets and gas masks, and sat with our feet on the skids as the choppers swooped in. The RAF boys were all dressed in their NBC (nuclear, biological, and chemical warfare) suits, and we staged a pitched battle on the grounds of the airport – thrilling stuff to me as a novice.

About halfway through our deployment, Prince Charles – who is the regiment's Colonel-in-Chief – came to visit us. We performed a casualty evacuation exercise for him at one of the British training areas in the Grunewald

Forest, and for the purposes of the exercise the officer in charge asked for a volunteer to be the casualty. This would mean being casevaced out in a Huey. I stuck my hand straight up and was given the role.

Five or six of us climbed into the back of an open-topped Land Rover and drove through the training area. I was operating the general-purpose machine-gun, and was scanning the horizon for potential threats. Suddenly there was an enormous bang from a thunderflash – a mock-up IED – and loads of smoke grenades started spewing out thick smoke. Within minutes the Huey was there. The medics moved me onto a stretcher and into the aircraft, and I was airlifted over the Grunewald.

My ears were ringing from the noise of the thunder-flash. But otherwise I was entirely unscathed. It was just an exercise, after all. Back at base everyone talked about the novelty of it all. The exercise had been a bit different from our usual regime, and doing it in front of Prince Charles had been a bonus. In retrospect, it all seems so innocent, because real-life casevacs are very far from exciting. And I sometimes wonder what, if I could go back in time and talk to that teenage lad, I would say to him. Would I tell him that before the year was out, he and his mates would be trundling along a road in circumstances eerily similar to those of that exercise? Would I tell him that there would be no royalty on hand to clap, or beers in the mess with the lads at the end of the day? Would I tell him that a thunderflash and a few smoke grenades could never prepare him for what was to come?

Or would I say nothing, and let him enjoy those last few months of blissful ignorance of the brutal realities of war? Those last few months of being unscarred and unbroken. Of being ordinary.

Northern Ireland, where we would be deployed after my six-month tour of Berlin, would involve a kind of soldiering totally different from that for which we had trained. Normal soldiering generally meant being out in the countryside and in the woods; in the Province we'd be in the streets, in built-up areas and among civilians. This meant there were new techniques to be learned: dealing with riot situations and petrol bombs, evading snipers, and coping with an enemy in plain clothes who looked no different from any other man in the street.

We had to acquaint ourselves fully with the British Army's Rules of Engagement. These are the strict guidelines set in place by the military that determine where, when, how and against whom force may or may not be used. The Rules of Engagement for Northern Ireland were particularly complicated. We were given a wad of cards that stated what we could and could not do in all kinds of situations, which we had to commit to memory. Of course, it wasn't lost on any of us that the enemy we were up against – the IRA – had no rules of engagement of their own; or that as members of the military, with our uniforms and red berets, we would be prime targets for armed Republicans. But we paid close attention to the Rules of Engagement, because we'd heard stories of people breaching them in the heat of battle and ending up being court-martialled and imprisoned.

We were taught recognition techniques – how to recall and describe the dress and features of someone you've only glanced at for a split second, or how to remember the details and registration number of a suspicious car. We honed these techniques over and over again until they became almost instinctive. And we learned how to look out for anything unusual. Why is it quiet in the street today? Why is there nobody about? On the streets of Northern Ireland we would need to be constantly vigilant, and that fact was drummed into us during our tour of Berlin.

On deployment in the Province, everyone within the regiment would have a different role. You might be an anti-tank gunner, or a machine-gun operator, or in signals, or a medic. I was part of the search team. This meant our speciality would be to go into an area and search for anything unusual or, where a suspicious package had been reported, identify whether it was a bomb or an IED and if necessary call in the bomb disposal unit. I loved training for the search team. It meant handling every sort of explosive there was and familiarizing myself with all the many kinds of devices that had been used by the IRA. I was astonished by the ingenuity of their bomb-makers. Most of their explosive materials were home-made out of easily obtainable fertilizer. As for the devices, once you'd got your head around the simple mechanics of a bomb – a circuit with a power source and a switch – you could booby-trap practically anything. I learned how it was possible to take a simple clothes peg and insert two drawing pins inside the clip end to make contact points. You could arm that trigger by placing, say, a book cover between the drawing pins. The moment somebody lifts up the book, the pins touch and the circuit is completed. We learned how to make a simple tilt switch using a test tube, a bung, and a ball bearing or a drop of mercury. Place the ball bearing into the tube and insert the bung. Then insert two wires through the bung. If the test tube is at one angle, the ball bearing or mercury will stay harmlessly at the safe end. But as soon as it tilts, it will roll towards the two wires and complete the circuit. Bang!

A basic car bomb could be made using a Tupperware box, a magnet and an alarm clock. All you needed to do was wire the alarm clock up to act as a timer for a detonator when the alarm rings, then pack the box with homemade explosives and tape the magnet to the inside of the lid so that the whole unit would stick to the underside of a vehicle.

Nowadays the IEDs laid in places like Afghanistan are far more sophisticated, using lasers and other advanced technology. Back then the devices were a lot more Heath Robinson, but that didn't make them any less devastating, and my time training for the search team brought home to me that, in a dirty conflict like the Troubles in Northern Ireland, you could never assume that anything or anyone was safe. As I was to find out to my cost, however, vigilance isn't always enough.

When our time in Berlin was over, Scotty and Dylan – good friends I'd made in the battalion – and I made our own way back to the UK, taking a train through East Germany to Frankfurt, then back across Europe, passing through Switzerland, France, Luxembourg, and Belgium. A little holiday. A happy time. And in the brief period of leave I had before our departure for Northern Ireland I went home to Nottingham and started going out with a girl called Claire, whom I'd known since my schooldays. This was a bit of a rarity. Not many of the guys had girl-friends, because our lives were so unsettled and so dominated by the Army – first during training in Aldershot, then on deployment in Berlin.

Life seemed good, and I was looking forward to the future.

By the time the battalion arrived in Northern Ireland in July 1979, the Troubles had been blazing for over a decade. In fact there had been tensions between Protestants and Catholics in the area for almost three centuries, but it was in 1968 that things deteriorated dramatically. It was in that year that members of the Northern Ireland Civil Rights Association, a Catholic body, marched through Londonderry in defiance of a government ban. A number of the protesters were injured by the RUC – the Royal Ulster Constabulary – that day, and this was the catalyst that sparked an increasingly devastating spiral of violence. Protestant and Catholic militants took to the streets of Belfast and Londonderry, leading to the Battle of Bogside – a two-day conflict between the Catholics and the RUC during which almost 1,500 people were injured.

The Northern Ireland government requested the help of the British Army in late 1969, and at first the soldiers were largely welcomed by the Catholic population. That didn't last. The perception soon arose that the police and the military were more on the side of the Protestants than the Catholics, and the situation in Northern Ireland became more and more volatile – a three-way war between the unionist Catholics who wanted a united Ireland, the loyalist Protestants who wanted the Province to remain part of the United Kingdom, and the police and military, whose role it was to keep the peace but who soon became an integral part of this political struggle. British soldiers became accustomed to angry taunts from both the Catholic and the Protestant communities. They could deal with that. But everyone knew it would only be a matter of time before a member of the security forces was killed in Northern Ireland. That day arrived on 6 February 1971, when Gunner Robert Curtis, of the Royal Artillery, was shot during a riot in Belfast.

Robert Curtis's death changed everything. When Brian Faulkner became the new Prime Minister of Northern Ireland the following month, he declared war on the IRA. Internment – the practice of holding prisoners without trial – was introduced. The violence escalated. More troops died – and more civilians too – and the sectarianism grew worse. One Catholic girl, treacherous enough to go out with a British soldier, had her hair shaved before being tarred and feathered and tied to a lamp-post. That March three squaddies went home with some girls they'd met in the pub. A Republican death squad was waiting for them.

At the beginning of 1970 the IRA had split into two wings: the official IRA and the new Provisional IRA, or 'Provos', who were more aggressive and militant. During 1971 there were more than 1,000 bombings, and while the British forces were obliged to stick to their Rules of Engagement and only fire when they were fired upon, the Provos used whatever tactics they could to gain an advantage.

The Parachute Regiment had been deployed in Northern Ireland in the early 1970s. On 30 January 1972 an event occurred that would again deepen the Troubles, be for ever written in the history books of the Paras, and enter the public consciousness on both sides of the sectarian divide. That event came to be known as Bloody Sunday.

What really happened that day is a matter of dispute, and it's not up to me to argue the rights and wrongs. All I know is that on that day an enormous protest march, 30,000 strong, was planned to pass through the streets of Londonderry – or Derry, as the Catholic majority in that town call it. At that time, Derry was a divided city. There was a 'line of containment' – an invisible border beyond which the security forces seldom dared to go. On the edge of this was an area known as Aggro Corner, from where young Republicans would hurl petrol bombs at the British forces. The Army had erected barricades along the line of containment, past which the protesters were not allowed to march. Some did, and a riot ensued, during which the Paras were given the order to fire with live rounds. Thirteen marchers – including seven teenagers – were killed that day; another man died a few months later of his injuries.

Bloody Sunday became a defining moment in the Troubles. As I write this, nearly forty years later, it is still written deep in the memory of those who were affected by it. Many millions of pounds were spent on an inquiry which lasted twelve years and concluded in 2010 that the Paras were at fault for firing into the crowd that day. I have mixed feelings about this finding. For the young men in Northern Ireland, the conflict was a new kind of war – a war in which you couldn't tell who was your friend and who was your enemy. When you join the Army you expect to have an enemy you can at least recognize, in a uniform that you can identify. Northern Ireland was very different from that. It was common for British troops to be shot at by plain-clothes snipers; the sniper would immediately pass the weapon on to an accomplice, who would run off with it and pass it on again. In circumstances like that, it's no wonder the Paras were jumpy on Bloody Sunday. I've no doubt that they reacted in as professional a way as they possibly could. After Bloody

Sunday, the training for British troops serving in Northern Ireland became more intense, the procedures more clearly defined. But Derry and Belfast were scary places, and to me it's a shame that British troops were put in that position in the first place.

I was just a child at the time, not even yet an Army Cadet. But Bloody Sunday affected me too, because from that day on the Parachute Regiment was the bête noire of the IRA. Anything they could do to take one of us out would be cause for celebration.

Our period of leave between Berlin and Northern Ireland was brief – just a couple of weeks. Back home in Nottingham, my mum seemed perfectly resigned to the idea of me going to the Province. I don't remember any great anxiety, no tears or displays of emotion. She was far more concerned about my plans to buy a motorbike, for which I'd been scrupulously saving. When she heard about that, she *did* wring her hands and beg me to reconsider, and I agreed, just to stop her from fretting.

Nor do I recall being nervous about my new posting. I've no memory of what incidents in Northern Ireland had been particularly newsworthy in the early months of 1979. For a start, I'd been abroad, but I was also just a young lad with my mind on matters other than current affairs. Perhaps I'd glance at the news headlines now and then, but I certainly wasn't the type to read the paper cover to cover. So when the time came for me to leave, no big fuss was made. I hugged my mum and my sisters, shook my brother by the hand and made my way to the station, where I caught a train to Liverpool. It was great to meet up with the lads again and take a ferry across the water. We were all looking forward to putting our training into action, and ready for our next adventure.

The battalion was stationed in Ballykinler, a small village on the coast in County Down. It's the most breathtaking location – three miles of desolate beach, with the granite peaks of the Mountains of Mourne in the background. Very out of the way, but that suited me fine. Ballykinler was home to an old army camp that had a long history. It had been a training camp during both World Wars, and during the Irish War of Independence it was controversially used as an internment camp. In 1974 the Provisional IRA planted a 300-pound bomb on the site, killing two soldiers and destroying some of the buildings.

From Ballykinler, we would be deployed down into 'Bandit Country'. This was the nickname given to the southern part of County Armagh. To look at it, you would never think this was one of the most dangerous postings in the world for a British soldier. It's a beautiful place: lush green fields, rugged moorland, rolling hills, and impressive mountains. There were no big cities in South Armagh – just small villages that felt as if they hadn't changed much in recent times. It's no wonder the people who live there are so fiercely protective of their homeland.

But the peace and gentleness of the landscape were deceptive. Nestled against the border with the Republic, this part of Northern Ireland had always been proudly Republican. It was a hotbed of IRA activity and a front line in the battle between them and the security forces. In the winding lanes of South Armagh, we could expect to be shot at, mortared, bombed. The area close to the border became known as the 'Murder Circle', because during the Troubles nearly 400 people lost their lives in this dangerous stretch of country. And of all the British soldiers killed by the IRA during the first ten years of the Troubles, nearly half died in South Armagh.

The role of the British Army in Bandit Country was to back up the police force and to be a visible sign of the rule of law. The duties of 2 Para were varied, and we rotated between different roles. We would be deployed to various fortifications and watchtowers down on the border; we would man vehicle checkpoints; we'd do escort duties and training exercises; and we'd perform patrols. Most of our patrolling was done on foot. This was for a good reason. The South Armagh branch of the IRA were specialists in roadside bomb ambushes. From my training in West Berlin I knew that to create a devastating bomb was alarmingly simple. The IRA knew that too. They placed their bombs in locations that they knew British soldiers were likely to pass, and they employed special scouts to record the security forces' regular activities, so they knew where we were likely to be, and when. So travelling by vehicle was particularly dangerous. To the IRA it was simplicity itself to put a bomb in a culvert under the road or in a roadside ditch, where it could remain for weeks without being noticed. It became so dangerous to travel overland through South Armagh that most Army deliveries were made by helicopter into an airfield that had been set up in the small village of Bessbrook. And it was because vehicle travel was so hazardous that we tended to patrol more often on foot. There was still a risk of sniper fire, but it meant that we could vary our routes more easily and not fall prey to the Provos' booby-traps.

During our training we had been shown a book that contained gruesome pictures of injured men. There was blood and gore everywhere, and bodies halfway between life and death. I remember looking at an image of a guy with a gunshot wound to the head and averting my eyes in disgust. My friends did the same. Revolted though we were by these pictures, we didn't allow ourselves to be worried by them. Traumas like that had nothing to do with us. They were the kind of thing you would have expected to see in Vietnam, where there had been a *real* war. But in the UK? No way.

Looking back, it seems naive, but although we all knew that South Armagh was a potentially dangerous place to be, I don't think any of us seriously thought we'd come to harm in Northern Ireland. Or if we did, we certainly never talked about it. Even the medical staff in the battalion, and the training NCOs who'd served previous tours in the Province, tended not to speak about the possibility of injury. It was taboo, off limits, something you just didn't discuss back then. When a soldier goes on active duty, he doesn't allow thoughts of what the enemy might do to him to prey on his mind. He can't. Otherwise he'd never do anything.

We weren't stupid. We knew there was the potential for rounds to be flying. We knew there was a likelihood of explosive devices – we'd been trained to search for them, after all. But for the first couple of months of our deployment in South Armagh everything seemed remarkably calm. No rounds were fired in anger; there were no bombs; we didn't even have exposure to any anti-British feeling, and as far as I knew, that was true for the whole of 2 Para. All the little jobs I went on ran smoothly.

It seems strange to say it now, but I enjoyed myself during those first two months. I remembered the motto of No.1 Parachute Training School – 'Knowledge Dispels Fear' – and it was true. I felt that I'd been equipped with the right knowledge to counter anything that might come along, and I was too young – too green, I suppose – to worry about death or injury.

Some events cannot be predicted. Some horrors are too dreadful to imagine. They come without warning, out of the blue, when you're looking the other way. And it doesn't matter how long life has been uneventful. It doesn't matter how prepared you are, or confident in your abilities. Sometimes it only takes a moment for life to change beyond recognition.

Knowledge might well dispel fear. But had I known that what was around the corner would be worse than any of the gory images of wounded soldiers we had been shown, I don't doubt that I would have been filled with the kind of fear that no knowledge in the world could ever dispel.

Chapter Four

Warrenpoint

Monday, 27 August 1979 was a hot, sunny bank holiday. The kind of day that would, in other circumstances, make you glad to be near the sea. Perhaps if it had been overcast, Earl Mountbatten of Burma, one of the Royal Navy's most prestigious officers, might not have decided to go fishing.

Lord Mountbatten had a holiday home in Mullaghmore, County Sligo, on the north-west coast of Ireland. He had a 30-foot boat, the *Shadow V*, moored unguarded in the harbour of that small seaside village, and it was his custom to go lobster-potting in Donegal Bay. The Irish police warned him not to go out on his boat that day, but he decided it would be safe. He was wrong. The previous night a member of the IRA had slipped on board the boat and planted a fifty-pound bomb with a remote-control detonator. The following day, together with members of his family and a small crew, Mountbatten set off looking for lobsters.

He never found them. As the *Shadow V* headed for Donegal Bay, a second IRA man detonated the device. Mountbatten wasn't killed instantly: he was severely wounded and perished soon after by drowning. Three others were killed in the blast: his 14-year-old grandson, his daughter's mother-in-law, and a 15-year-old crew member. It was a terrible atrocity, and would have been enough for that bank holiday Monday to go down as one of the darkest days of the Troubles. But it wasn't over yet.

As part of A Company, my mates and I were due to relieve 2 Para's Support Company at the town of Newry in County Down, just near the county border with Armagh. The Troubles had hit Newry hard, with several fatalities over the previous few years, and the Paras' role there was to reinforce the police presence. As far as we were concerned, it was just another day on rotation, and we spent the morning in camp at Ballykinler, preparing to be transported down to Newry.

It was the habit of our commanders at Ballykinler to work out different possible routes between two points. That way we could select routes at random and increase our chances of thwarting the IRA scouts that we knew were trying to identify which roads we were most likely to use, and when. The route that was selected for our journey that day was to take us south on the A2, along the coast, before heading west along the estuary of Carling-ford Lough, through the town of Warrenpoint, and up into Newry. Of all the routes we could take, this was possibly the most dangerous, because just above

Warrenpoint the estuary thinned at a place called Narrow Water. On the other side of the estuary was the Republic of Ireland, where thick forest ran down to the coast. From the IRA's point of view, it was a good place for an ambush, because they could lie hidden in wait on the Republic's side of the water with a clear view of the traffic passing on our side, detonate a bomb by remote control, and instantly disappear. Moreover, this was the route that a Royal Marine patrol took in a Land Rover fairly frequently to check on a nearby container terminal. But to avoid this route entirely would just make it more likely that we'd be hit on one of the alternative routes. We had to keep the enemy guessing.

There were three vehicles that were to take A Company to Newry that day: two four-ton lorries and a Land Rover. Nowadays soldiers in war zones are – quite rightly – given vehicles that are specially designed to withstand the blast of an IED, but there was nothing unusually robust about these vehicles. And as my mates and I got ready to leave, we put on our flak vests, but we also donned our red berets rather than wearing helmets. Partly this was out of defiance, but there was another reason for us not to want to look too heavily armed. In the eyes of large parts of the population of Northern Ireland, we were an occupying force. We were all very mindful of the battle for hearts and minds, and we knew that if we appeared too aggressive it would make that battle harder to win.

'Hurry up and wait!' is an expression you hear a lot in the British Army, and there was a lot of hanging around that day, waiting to get the order to leave Ballykinler and set off for Newry. We were going to be stationed in the town for some time, so we had all our bags packed and ready to go, and I remember killing time in the little 'choggy shop', or café, at base, playing with the lads on the Space Invaders machine – the latest thing at the time. It was very hot and everyone was impatient to get off, as well as a little bit anxious about the dangers of heading down along the border. Finally we were ready to leave: Woody, Jonesy, Dylan and I climbed up into one of the four-tonners together, along with Tom Caughy, Private Gary Barnes, whom everyone called Barney, and one other guy from a different platoon. Corporal Johnny Giles was driving.

There were only eight of us in our vehicle, six in the back, two in the front, because we were also carrying the company ammunition – boxes of rifle rounds, mortar rounds, grenades, link for the machine-gun. It was mid-afternoon when we set off. I can't remember who was sitting next to me, but I know that I was at the back of the lorry, on the tailgate, my rifle at the ready so I could keep a lookout for anything suspicious. Tom changed seats with Barney, a close friend of his who'd been with him in the junior company. Barney was a real character. Good fun. Solid. He was struggling with the exhaust fumes that were pumping into the lorry, so Tom offered to swap places. Our three-vehicle convoy trundled out of Ballykinler, and although we were just shooting the breeze in our usual way, we were all finding it unbearably hot and just wanted to get to our destination.

That is the last memory I have of the day that was to change so many people's lives for ever. And it is the last memory six of my friends and colleagues in that truck would ever have.

I can only relate the horrors of the next few hours by piecing together what other people have told me.

It was a little before five o'clock when our platoon of approximately twenty-six soldiers approached Warrenpoint. Our convoy had reached the dual carriageway that ran alongside Narrow Water, and was passing a lay-by where a lorry loaded with bales of hay was parked up. The lorry contained an 800-pound fertilizer bomb, packed in beer kegs and attached to a radio-controlled detonator. As far as I know, the IRA had set up this roadside bomb in the hope of hitting one of the Marine patrols that used this road regularly. When they saw a company of red berets coming – the devils of Bloody Sunday – they must have been doing somersaults of joy at their luck.

The lorry in which my mates and I were travelling was the last one in the convoy. The first two passed the roadside bomb safely. It was as our vehicle drew alongside it that two Provos, safely hidden on the other side of the estuary, detonated the device.

The noise must have been enormous, but I have no memory of it, or of any of the events that followed.

Our truck was hurled onto its side and into the central reservation, its chassis ripped apart, a wrecked, mangled heap of burning metal. The ammunition that we were carrying started to ignite, causing hundreds of tiny explosions. Bodies were flung from the wreckage and into the road. Johnny Giles lay slumped across the steering wheel as if sleeping. He would never wake up. The air filled with the sound of the screams of the wounded and the smell of burning flesh, which most likely included mine. My body was on fire in the minutes after the explosion. I lay there unconscious in the searing heat while the skin on my face and arms charred and my legs burned to the bone.

As soon as the bomb exploded, the Land Rover in front crossed the central reservation of the A2 and spun round so that it was facing the way it came. The other lorry found cover under some nearby trees. Confusion was everywhere. The surviving members of A Company heard the sound of our ammo detonating and assumed that a sniper was firing on them. And so they fired back, aiming their rounds across the narrow estuary towards the Republic. In doing so, they killed one innocent civilian and injured another.

Our platoon commander desperately tried to raise HQ on the radio, but for some reason the radio communications were down. Fortunately a Wessex helicopter picked up the platoon commander's call and relayed what had happened to HQ. The chopper was given the order to pick up a medical team and a quick-reaction force, then immediately return to Warrenpoint. Firefighters were on the scene in minutes to help put out the flames, including those that were eating up my own flesh.

As soon as word of the blast reached Newry, a quick-reaction force comprising two Land Rovers full of Paras was immediately dispatched to the site. In addition Lieutenant Colonel David Blair of the Queen's Own Highlanders, who happened to be in the air in a small helicopter at the time, diverted to the scene.

In the Army there are standard operating procedures, or SOPs – instructions about what to do under certain circumstances – and these were followed to the letter. On the other side of the road, perhaps 150 metres on from the blast point, there was a granite gate-lodge opposite the entrance to Narrow Water Castle, a well-known beauty spot. As the quick-reaction force, Lieutenant Colonel Blair, and our OC, Major Fursman, congregated at the blast site, they set up an incident control point inside the gate-lodge. It was the sensible thing to do as it was close to where they needed to be and could be easily defended if necessary.

However, the IRA's scouts had done their work well. They had studied the Army's SOPs. They knew that the gate-lodge was the most likely place to set up an incident control point, and so they had planted a second device there, hidden in some innocuous-looking milk pails. In terms of loss of life, this bomb would prove to be even more devastating than the first. The bombers, hidden on the other side of the water, detonated the second device just as the gate-lodge was full of soldiers.

The whole building collapsed. Chunks of rock the size of footballs shot through the air and landed almost 100 metres away. By this time I had been transferred to a Wessex. The chopper was just feet above the ground when its windows were blasted in as it attempted to casevac me and others to the safety of Musgrave Park Hospital in Belfast.

Nowadays we hear of bombings almost daily, of IEDs in Afghanistan or atrocities in Iraq. Perhaps we don't stop to think about what it really means. Even I find it hard to imagine what the sight of that massacre at Warrenpoint must have looked like. Hard to imagine the horror and even now, so many years later, hard to recount what I'm told it looked like. A part of me feels reluctant to do so. Narrow Water is a beauty spot, but there was nothing beautiful about it that day. There were two enormous craters where the two bombs had been located. Horrifically wounded men were strewn around the road. But worst of all, the area was littered with human body parts. Gobbets of flesh hung from trees, so far up that even the firemen's ladders were unable to reach them. Limbs lay in the grass verge and on the road. Entire torsos had been separated from legs. The same went for heads. The living were so appalled by the sight that many of them had to vomit into the bushes. And the blasts were so severe that some of the guys were never found. The epaulettes of his uniform were all that remained of Lieutenant Colonel David Blair; the rest of his body had been utterly destroyed. And when a dive team arrived, one of them made a gruesome discovery in the estuary. It was a human face, still recognizable as that of Major Fursman. It had been ripped whole from its owner's skull. The police said they had never seen such carnage as they witnessed that day.

It wasn't for many years that I ever discussed in detail the events at Warrenpoint with anybody who was there. It's not really the sort of thing that comes up easily in conversation. Decades later, however, I was at a function for limbless ex-servicemen overlooking the Thames at the House of Commons when a guy called Kev Bryant, whom I had known over the years and who had lost a leg doing mine-clearance in Angola, turned up. Kev had been to the funeral of a friend that day, and had a few beers at the wake, which made him more talkative than usual. He put his arm round me and confided that he'd been at Warrenpoint. I was stunned – I'd known him for years and he'd never mentioned anything about it, but perhaps that wasn't surprising. Like me, he was only 18 at the time, and new to the Army – an engineer on one of his first deployments. His job was to go round the bomb site with a large plastic bag, collecting limbs and bits of body. To be presented with such horror at such a young age hardly bears thinking about. Small wonder Kev had tried to forget about it. I can barely imagine how the rest of 2 Para coped with seeing their own mutilated like that.

Eighteen men died that day. Sixteen of them were from the Parachute Regiment, two from the Queen's Own Highlanders. Among the dead were my friends Woody and Jonesy – I had joined up with them and we had shared the kind of bond that only army mates can have – and

Dylan, who had become a close friend once we joined the battalion in West Berlin. Of the eight people in our truck, only two survived, myself and Tom. Tom's leg was damaged and he sustained terrible burns, but he knew he was only alive because he'd swapped seats with Barney.

The two bomb blasts at Warrenpoint that day saw the biggest loss of life in a single incident for the British Army, not only during the Troubles but since the end of the Second World War. The tragedy of the massacre was rather overshadowed by the death of Earl Mountbatten and his family, but not for the Parachute Regiment, which had now sustained the greatest loss of life of any unit in Northern Ireland. I can't imagine what the scenes back at Ballykinler would have been like in the days that followed, or the feelings of the families as they waited for word of their loved ones. My mother had the dreaded knock at the door, but the news was not the worst. What wives and children and parents must have felt like when they learned that their husbands and fathers and sons had died, and the manner of their death, is too painful for me to think about. I've heard that the IRA feared a brutal response from the regiment, revenge for the killings of their colleagues. No such response came and that is, I think, something to be proud of. Something that shows the professionalism of the regiment.

As for the survivors, casevaced immediately to hospital, nobody knew that day how serious their injuries would be. One thing was sure: for them there were very difficult times ahead. But when I think back on that day, on the sacrifice made by so many of my mates, and the brutal and tragic way in which they died, a single fact remains very clear to me: despite the pain and indignity of the months that were to follow, despite the tears and traumas, despite the awful reality that my life could never be the same again, I was one of the lucky ones.

Chapter Five

Broken

My brother John was a strong man, a former CID officer, and not given to overreaction. When he saw me for the first time after I was blown up, he was so horrified that he asked if it would not be kinder to let me die. I can understand why he said this. I was in bits. Wrecked. Only just alive.

My right foot was smashed up, the sole blown clean open and the heel missing; my left leg was in an even worse state. My hand was deeply sliced and the tip of one of my fingers was hanging off. My arm was broken at the elbow and large areas of my skin were horribly burned. I was taken to the Queen Elizabeth Military Hospital, a 400-bed hospital in Woolwich, south-east London. The doctors' first thoughts were for the burns I'd sustained, so I was placed into intensive care in the burns unit. The pungent, acrid, sickening smell of burned flesh which pervaded that ward will stay with me till I die. Most of my torso had been protected by the standard-issue flak vest I'd been wearing – nothing like the body armour the guys wear nowadays, but enough to give me some sort of protection. Even so, the skin on both my legs, and some on my shoulder and back, had been badly burned. There were also flash burns to other parts of my body – bad enough for all the skin to have peeled off my hands and face, but not so deep and damaging here as elsewhere. My eardrums were bust, all my hair had gone, I'd lost four teeth, and my chin was cut open.

My legs were swollen like tree trunks and the burns had gone down to the bone. They were black. Parts of my burned areas were covered with a gauze dressing, and I lay there with just a pillowcase draped over me to conceal my manhood. The room was kept very hot to promote healing, and everyone who came to visit had to wear a gown, a mask, gloves, and shoe covers. The doctors inserted drips into both arms and pipes into both nostrils so that they could get nutrition and water into me, but my weight still went down from twelve stone to about five. All in all, I looked pretty good.

During those early days and weeks, because of the pain and the drugs, the dehydration, and the shock my body was experiencing, I was totally out of it. My memory of the hours, days, and weeks that followed the Warrenpoint bombing are like a broken mirror: splintered. I can just recall little flashes, more like still photographs than real memories. I see myself on the ward of Musgrave Park Hospital. Margaret Thatcher visited us, but I was unconscious and missed her. I remember myself in a stretcher, hooked up in an aircraft. I don't know whether that was the chopper that casevaced me out of the blast site or the aircraft bringing me back to the mainland. There were days on end when I saw nothing but the lights on the ceiling and the occasional masked face looking down at me.

I was out of it for several weeks. My mum tells me I swore and cursed at her, but I have no memory of that; I was just dipping in and out of consciousness, bewildered by everything that was happening. So I don't know how long I had been there when a doctor entered the ward with a solemn look on his face. I had just emerged from a period of unconsciousness, and had no way of knowing how long it had been, or what had happened in that time.

The doctor took a seat next to my bed. 'Paul,' he said, his brow slightly furrowed. 'You need to prepare yourself for some bad news.'

I gave him a confused look, unable to move because of my sore and broken body. Given the state I was in, what more bad news could there be?

'The injuries to your left leg were just too severe,' he carried on. 'We've had to amputate it.'

At first I was in too much of a daze to take in fully what he said, or even to react; and I was just too poorly to feel angry, frustrated, or otherwise upset. But gradually, like water soaking into the parched earth, the reality started to sink in, and I felt as though the building of my life was crumbling around me.

Ever since I was a boy, I'd felt as if everything had been planned out. I'd written my life off to the Army, and was always going to be a soldier, travelling the world, doing the job I loved. It was all I wanted. But how could I do that now? How could anything ever be the same again? I felt as if I hadn't just lost a limb: I'd lost my reason for being. My purpose. When the doctor gave me that shocking news in that bleak, stinking little hospital room, I truly felt as if my life had stopped.

It wasn't until much later that I realized how lucky I was that they took off only one leg, and that the amputation was just below the knee. It's much better for an amputation to take place below the joint because then you have the manoeuvrability of that joint. An above-the-knee amputation means that you only have the use of the hip joint, and need to use a mechanical knee, which makes life a lot more difficult.

Even though I kept my right leg, it was still very badly damaged. It has caused me constant pain ever since because, aside from the fact that the skin continually splits and breaks, I lost my heel. The sole was blown open, the tendons destroyed, and there were soft skin grafts where hard skin should be. When at last I was able to walk again, I was walking on the piece of bone that should have been covered by my heel. Even now I have the constant sensation that someone has hit me with a hammer on the sole of the foot. There was always – and there remains – the possibility of amputating the right foot. On balance, though, I think it's better to put up with the pain and to manage my life around it, because having that foot makes a big difference to me. It means, for example, that when I drive a car I can actually feel the accelerator and the brake. Over the years I would meet lots of double amputees and come to realize that losing both legs is a whole other ball game.

I'm told that rather than focus on my legs, I became obsessed with the state of my teeth and mouth. I'd lost the front four teeth, which were now just broken stumps, and my chin and upper lip were cut open. I guess my brain just had to focus on something simple to stay in control.

Day and night I had painkillers and antibiotics pumped into me. I also underwent a long series of skin grafts, and my memory is that these were more painful than the burns themselves, because lots of the nerves in my legs had been scorched away. The operation involved taking a razor sharp implement, a bit like something you'd use to plane wood, and slicing thin strips of skin from my back one week, then my chest, and when those bits of me were too sore to touch they moved on to my upper arms, or any other bit of me that wasn't burned. What the medics took off was thin enough that the skin would grow back from where they'd removed it. They would then lay these pieces of skin over a burned area, cover it with a gauze dressing, and hope that it would all take. Today the skin of my right leg and the stump of my left are like a patchwork quilt made over a painstaking period of weeks by those skilled doctors thirty years ago.

It was indescribably painful having those sheets of skin planed from my body. Each time the nurses removed my dressing my body would shake uncontrollably with agony. To help the healing process, I had to take saline baths. The nurses would wheel me out on a special trolley and slowly lower me part of the way down; then the whole bath would be raised up, submerging my raw body into the salt water. That too caused me excruciating pain, but this was followed by a strange kind of pleasure as the healing water did its work.

In many ways I think that period must have been more horrific for my mum and the rest of the family – who of course had come down to Woolwich to see me – than it was for me. My mum was able to stay in one of the Red Cross flats on the site of the hospital so that she could be near me. She was, by all accounts, hysterical at first, and my sisters, who lived close by, had to look after her in those early days. In the beginning they would come and see me every day, then two or three times a week. I only remember them being full of smiles and pleased to see me, though I've no doubt that, away from the ward, my mum especially would have cried the tears that only a mother seeing her child on the brink of death can know. I was so grateful for their presence, though. They were my lifeline, my link to the outside world, as were the other friends and strangers who visited. Friends came down from Nottingham, and they would bring *their* friends. Jo and Amanda Knatchbull – the grandchildren of Lord Mountbatten – came to visit several times, which was a great honour. They even invited me to their grandfather's memorial service at St Paul's Cathedral. I borrowed a red beret and a uniform, but I'd lost so much weight that the clothes hung off me. I was taken to St Paul's in a wheelchair with my foot wrapped in enormous bandages. I looked a fright as I was carried in my wheelchair up the steps of the cathedral, but it was a moving experience, and I felt touched that the Mountbatten family had remembered me. Years later Timothy Knatchbull, whose twin brother died in the Mountbatten blast, came to visit me. It was very cathartic for us both to be able to talk about our memories of that day.

In those early days the sight of me must have been terrible for all my visitors. I was too out of it to fully understand what was going on, whereas they had a ring-side view of my burned and broken body. Much later I would see clinical photographs of what I looked like. I can fully understand why my brother John made the comment that he did.

There are moments in my life that my brain has not allowed me to remember. Moments too traumatic to hold onto. Learning about the loss of my mates is one of those. I have only the haziest recollection of discovering that Woody, Jonesy, Dylan, Barney and the others were dead. Gradually, though, the reality sank in, and it was as if my battered body had another set of agonizing blows to absorb.

Young people do not often experience death, and when they do it is frequently in the form of an elderly relative passing away after a long and active life. I find it hard to explain how I felt in those early days about the death of my three close friends, and all the others who died that day. Hard to describe the grief, or the emptiness. There were moments when I vowed to go over to Northern Ireland and kill every member of the IRA to avenge the slaughter of my friends. Then the anger would pass, and I'd be left with just the sorrow. Young, optimistic men, full of enthusiasm and promise, with their lives ahead of them, were gone. It seemed impossible. Unreal. Their deaths had left a hole in the lives of those who knew them, an emptiness that could never be filled. The sense of loss was unspeakable. The anguish intolerable. I mourned each one of those deaths and I still do. The private, tearful moments I spent immobile in my hospital bed would not ease with the passage of time.

I did what I could to remember the happy times we spent together. The months in training, all of us suffering together as we tabbed across the countryside in training, covered in mud and drenched, or endured the ordeal of P Company. I tried to keep the good moments at the front of my mind, to cherish the memories in an attempt to block out the awful reality. But inevitably the clouds would sometimes descend on my mind. I wasn't the type to share these thoughts with people, so I kept them buttoned up, stashed away in a little box in my head where I knew they would remain for the rest of my life.

It was the only way I knew how to move on and stay positive.

Grief was not the only emotion I had to deal with. I had survived, but only just. There was no reason, other than chance, that I was alive and they were dead. I was good friends with some of the men who had died, even though we had been together for only a short time; others I didn't know at all. It didn't really make much difference either way. There is a sense of guilt that goes hand in hand with being a survivor. A shame almost. As if you've been given a second chance that you deserve no more than those who didn't make it. Even today the guilt is always there. A constant companion to my fortunate life.

It wasn't just me that was overcome by this feeling of guilt. In the aftermath of the Warrenpoint bombings, a travel agent donated a holiday for the next of kin of those eighteen soldiers who had died, as well as the families of those who had been seriously injured. So it was that my mum found herself in Tenerife along with the families of the dead. It must have been very difficult for all them, being alongside each other: difficult for the bereaved to be with the families of those who had made it, and vice versa. Mum was of course relieved that I had lived, but she too felt that overpowering sense of guilt that comes with being a survivor. Some of the other families took out their frustration and grief on my mum. She was reduced to tears and desperately wanted to be by my bedside. Even then, she wasn't sure that I would survive.

The battalion, of course, was still in Northern Ireland during the time I was hospitalized, and still had more than a year to go there, so I didn't really get to see a lot of the guys or to share my grief with them. The Parachute Regiment was my second family, and not to be with them at this emotional time was extraordinarily painful. Some of those who had been injured in the second blast were recuperating in hospital in Woolwich, but they were in a different ward. One of them, I found out after a while, was Norrie Porter, the corporal who, the day we'd arrived in Berlin, had given us money to go down to the NAAFI. Norrie's injuries were particularly bad. When the second blast had gone off, he'd got a lump of granite in the head. As a result, he was paralysed down one side. Another guy, whom we called Spider Web, was spattered with granite, his head and face smashed, an eye gone, and an arm needing to be rebuilt. They took over a pound of granite from his thigh.

I did everything I could to keep my chin up, but that's not to say there weren't some very dark moments. For the first few weeks I was confined to an intensive-care bay and was simply too poorly even to feel down. As I started the slow process of recovery, I was placed with Tom, the other survivor from the first blast, and the only Para on the ward with me. Tom hadn't sustained the same kind of bone damage that I had, but his wounds were still very severe. One of his ankles was badly smashed and his backside and legs were burned, which, as you can imagine, caused a lot of pain and discomfort. And having only survived because he'd changed places with Barney, he had the mental scars to deal with too. Tom was up and gone from the hospital quite a time before me, but while we were together in a four-man bay it was good for our morale. And if there was one thing I needed, it was a morale boost.

The recovery process would take a long, painful time. I struggled not to be frustrated with the slowness of the treatment and the intensity of the pain I was in. Sometimes I found myself bargaining in my head. If only I could have lost an arm, I would think, instead of a leg. Then at least I'd be able to move around and be of more use. But then the cold reality would hit me. There was no point bargaining. Nothing was going to change.

It being a military hospital – with all the banter and the gallows humour that comes with it – sympathy could sometimes be a bit thin on the ground. It wasn't long after my leg had been amputated that a male nurse told me I needed to have another saline bath. Before I was lowered into the salt water, he needed to remove the gauze dressing from my stump. It was agonizing, because what remained of my leg had almost grown into the dressing, but the nurse – in true military style – was somewhat gung-ho about removing it. 'A bit of pain never hurt anyone' was his attitude. I was almost crying. I ended up bashing my bloodied stump in the guy's nose, an involuntary movement because of the pain, obviously. He upped and left the room. I never saw him again.

I have a memory of lying in my hospital bed during the early days, covered only with that pillowcase, when a couple of people – I don't remember who – wandered in. They lifted up the pillowcase and sniggered at what they found underneath it, which were very swollen, like tennis balls. Then they scuttled away, giggling.

Everything was such an effort. As I'd lost so much weight, I had to drink Complan-style drinks to build me up. It seemed that every half an hour they were putting another one of these things in front of me. I still had pipes in my nose, so sipping these horrible things would make me retch, which forced the pipe out. In the end they all had to come out to stop the gagging reflex, then the nurses would have to reinsert them all. It was all so uncomfortable and undignified. Each time I had to swallow one of the interminable pills the doctors gave me, it was like swallowing a rock because my throat was so sore. A simple thing like that would use up so much energy it left me totally exhausted. Most of the early days were spent lying on my back, apart from when the nurses used a special surgical bed to turn me over onto my front. This involved sandwiching the mattress around me and rolling the whole bed over, and was painful enough. But sitting up was even worse. All the blood would rush to the lower half of my body, causing a terrible burning sensation in my legs. And when the time first came for me to move to an orthopaedic chair, it felt like my blood was on fire. I'd be sitting in this horrible, uncomfortable, plastic seat, propped up by cushions, just staring at the clock, begging for the time to arrive when I could get back into bed.

A dietician used to come up from the kitchens with a little clipboard and ask me what I wanted to eat. I could have anything, she told me. *Anything.* If I'd asked for grilled lobster and Beef Wellington, they'd have got it for me. But all I could even contemplate eating was mashed potato, or maybe some soup or ice cream. Anything else was too much of an effort. And of course by the time my appetite was back and I *was* fit enough to choose whatever my heart desired, the offer was no longer there and I was back on hospital rations. I had a similar issue when Prince Charles, in his capacity as the Parachute Regiment's Colonel-in-Chief, sent me and all those who were injured an enormous hamper of exotic fruit from one of the posh London stores. It looked amazing, but with tubes shoved down my nose and unable to eat anything, I wasn't really in a state to enjoy his generosity. The one thing in the hamper that did catch my interest, though, was a bottle of malt whisky. I gave it to my mum to look after until I was well enough to drink it. Months later, when I was still in hospital, I said to Mum, 'You know, I wouldn't mind a drop of that malt whisky.'

Mum looked a bit embarrassed.

'That might be a bit difficult, Paul,' she said. It turned out she'd taken to putting a dram of the Prince's scotch into her coffee at night, and it was all gone. Given the stress she was under, I can't say I really blame her.

The physiotherapists were keen to get me moving as soon as possible. I'd been taken to Lord Mountbatten's memorial service, but I was very much bandaged up and confined to a wheelchair, and besides, I needed more than the occasional trip out. The physios wheeled me to the gymnasium part of the physiotherapy department where there were some parallel bars. 'Paul,' they told me, 'you need to hold onto the parallel bars and start hopping.'

I gave it a go, but almost crumpled with the pain even though my 'good' foot was wrapped in bandages and padding.

'It *really* hurts,' I breathed.

The physios shook their heads. 'Come on,' they said, their voices full of brusque encouragement. 'We've got to get you on your feet, we've got to get you walking again.'

So I tried again, putting the pressure on my foot as I pushed myself to hop and hobble along while gripping the parallel bars. I hadn't gone more than a few paces when my foot started to bleed profusely, and it wouldn't stop. I was standing in a puddle of blood, which was when the physios decided that perhaps I wasn't quite ready to be doing exercises of this type after all.

Hand in hand with the physical pain and the difficulties it presented came the psychological trauma. I can't honestly say that I felt much self-pity at what had happened. How could I, when so many people had lost their lives? I knew, deep down, that I had no right to complain about what had happened to me: I was still there, and they weren't. Knowing what the families of those men would have sacrificed to have their sons, husbands and fathers back, even with injuries like mine, made it impossible for me to feel sorry for myself. Even from those earliest days in hospital I was very clear that I had to use the life that I had to make up, somehow, for their loss. To be constructive about the situation, rather than depressed.

There were, however, difficult barriers to overcome. Every day was a physical and mental effort to get well. I just wanted to be out of that place. I felt as though I ought to be moving on, doing something positive with my life instead of being stuck in hospital, day after day, week after week, month after month. Despite the extremely difficult nature of those first few months of recovery, both Tom and I did what we could to be positive and not feel sorry for ourselves. In some respects that was easier than it might sound, because there was a constant stream of other patients in our ward to remind us that we weren't the only people in difficulty.

Although it was a military hospital, a certain proportion of the patients came from the local population. A 60-year-old tramp by the name of Eugene Maguire arrived one day. He'd been living in Epping Forest, and the story was that he'd been smoking a roll-up cigarette and drinking meths at the same time. Not a good combination: I've never in my life seen somebody so badly burned. His nose was just a stump, he had the stump of a single ear, and his eyelids had burned away. He'd lost the hand from one arm, which was now shrivelled tight to his

chest; on the other hand he had just the stumps of his
fingers and thumbs. The poor guy was in a bay with Tom
and me, and he was as hard as nails. As soon as the doctors
had done his skin grafts, and the Red Cross had given him
a new suit of clothes and a wig, he was off. The police
would bring him back again, speechless with alcohol, and
despite his injuries, he was able to roll and light a cigarette with the stumps of the fingers on his damaged hand.
He disappeared again and that was the last we saw of him;
but seeing somebody in such a terrible state made us
aware that in fact our injuries could have been a lot worse.

Another bloke had come off his motorbike and lost a
load of flesh from his legs. The doctors decided to do a
thick skin graft from his stomach, but they weren't able
simply to cut off the skin and layer it on the leg like they
had done with me because the flesh on the stomach was
too thick and the skin itself would have died if it had
been removed from a blood source. Instead, once they had
removed the skin that was to be grafted, they made a tube
of flesh, connected one end of this to the body, grafted
the skin onto it, then hooked the whole thing up to one of
his arms to ensure a supply of blood. The poor chap was
confined to bed for the entire time I was in hospital,
unable to move because of the positioning of his skin
graft, which the doctors only disconnected from his arm
and applied to his leg after several weeks, once it had
developed its own blood supply. And then, some months
later when I had to go back to hospital for a check-up, he
was there again. The doctors had had to remove his leg:

after all that, the skin graft had failed. Some people might feel hard done by. Not him. You never heard him complain or moan or feel sorry for himself. That, in itself, was an inspiration.

There was a fusilier who had been to Northern Ireland six times and been injured by the IRA seven times. While I was there he was recuperating from a bullet in the knee. He married a staff nurse – hardly surprising, really, given the amount of time he'd spent in a hospital ward.

Six firemen arrived one day. They'd been fighting a fire in London when some acetylene canisters had ignited and exploded. Their burns were terrible but, like Tom and me, they did what they could to keep their spirits up. Their mates would come in and visit, and when that happened it was party time: they'd bring cases of beer and bottles of wine that would end up secreted in bedside lockers or behind curtains. Now and then they'd slip us a can or two – no doubt against all the hospital's regulations. The doctors and nurses seemed happy enough to turn a blind eye to it, though, especially as the fridge in the ward kitchen was well stocked with Guinness – a bottle a day being part of our regime to help build us up again.

After a few months I started to get better and could move around the hospital in a wheelchair. Not being the kind of person who wants to stay still – especially having been bedridden for so long – I used to whizz around the wards visiting various people. A chap called Geoff Tuffin, who was a captain in the Para Engineers, had been hit by a tank on a training exercise. There wasn't a mark on his body, but he was almost entirely paralysed by the whip-lash. All he could move were his eyes. Often when people visit patients in hospital they are very sympathetic, perhaps overly sympathetic, with their kind words and bunches of grapes. But as Geoff was a military man like me, I knew he would be craving a bit of army gossip and humour, so I would sit at his bedside, just chatting to him and reminiscing about jump school and P Company in an attempt to make his days a bit less bleak. He was too ill to make any facial expressions, but I could tell just by the movement of his eyes that he felt better for my being there. Eventually he recovered enough to walk with help, and even married one of the ward sisters, Maggie.

With so many people suffering such terrible injuries, it was hard to feel sorry for yourself. In a place like that you didn't have to look far to find someone who was worse off than you were, and I found it difficult to complain about my lot when I saw people with much more debilitating injuries not saying a word. Sometimes it seemed the doctors tried to use that to medical advantage by putting people in our bay who weren't so badly hurt as Tom and I were. One young lad wanted to become a soldier but had a crucifix tattooed on his forehead. That had to go, so he was admitted to the Queen Elizabeth and placed on the burns and plastics ward, where we were being treated. I suppose that for him to see the state that the two of us were in must have been a sobering experience.

I was in that hospital for eleven months – long, difficult months during which time I had to gradually get used to the idea that my life was never going to be the same again. I did my best to keep positive, and looking back I don't remember feeling particularly down about my situation. Frustrated, yes; bored, certainly. It all seemed like such a terrible waste of time. My relationship with Claire stuttered on for a while, and she came down a few times to visit me. It soon petered out, but I was self-aware enough to realize that it probably would have done whether I'd been blown up or not. The last thing I wanted to do, though, was dwell on the negatives of my situation. I was young and eager to get on with my life, to be outside, running and having a good time. To get back to the regiment. All my mates – those who had survived – were still serving. I just wanted to be alongside them. It bit particularly hard when the Falklands conflict came along. The Parachute Regiment went off to the South Atlantic for the adventure of a lifetime, but of course I couldn't go with them. While I was hobbling round on crutches, they were at Goose Green, seeing plenty of action and doing what I'd always wanted to do ever since I was a little boy looking through the fence into the army training camp in Toton. And the frustration only increased once the pain of my burns and injuries subsided. I didn't feel especially ill, but I couldn't do all the things I wanted because my body was broken and wouldn't let me.

The support I received during my eleven months in the Queen Elizabeth Military Hospital was astonishing. I made lifelong friends there, and not just with other patients. An ex-officer from the Paras by the name of

John Haw lived nearby. I'd never met him before, but he would come in to see me once a week along with his wife Val, who had been an officer in the Queen Alexandra Royal Nursing Corps. At a time when the more visitors I received to break up the monotony of my recovery the better, their visits were more welcome than I could ever have told them, as were the visits of my brother and his family, and my sisters. When Christmas came I was well enough to be transported up to Nottingham to spend the time with my family. A ramp was erected outside our house so my wheelchair could get in and out. And I was astonished to discover the response my accident had brought out in the citizens of my home town. People from all round the city had carried out different fundraising events and raised £1,200 – a lot of money back then. I was taken into town, where a number of department stores had donated gift vouchers to help make my Christmas a little more festive. I had, after all, lost everything I owned in the bomb blast. They were small acts of kindness that went a long way to helping me get better.

As time passed, and my recovery progressed, I became more and more frustrated with my inability to move around with any freedom. The skin on my body was so tight from the skin grafts that I couldn't reach the lift buttons on the lift, but I was no longer ill – just broken – and so I took to whizzing round the hospital in my wheelchair, visiting the lads in the orthopaedic wards, or cheering up the kids in the paediatric ward. I had a bandage around my stump, and I used to draw a little face on it, which I could move around rather like a glove puppet. I named him Arfur – Arfur Leg – and it brought a few smiles to the kids who found themselves in hospital. One of the nurses came in one day having made for me a stump puppet with a sweet face and big, floppy ears. Looking back, half of me wonders if I might have traumatized those poor kids – but they seemed entertained at the time!

As soon as I could move about, I didn't stop. There were these enormous ramps that ran from the top floor of the hospital to the bottom, so the staff could wheel beds and trolleys up and down. I used to whoosh down those ramps, doing crazy handbrake turns. The wheelchairs we had in those days were pretty basic – push them too hard and they'd soon start growing rickety – so whenever I passed a wheelchair in the corridor that looked better than mine, I'd swap, after checking none of the nurses was watching. In the end I was getting through about a wheelchair a week. My mum remembers me trying to do handstands on my wheelchair, with my stump and other leg all bandaged up – all part of a planned campaign to make people in the hospital smile. On another occasion I'd been on one of my visits to the children's ward to try to cheer up all the sick kids. The matron had a glass-windowed office just outside the ward, and Mum recalls cringing with embarrassment as she saw me pass that office, slumped down in my seat so the matron couldn't see me through the window, with a little train of kiddies' bikes attached to the wheelchair as I sneaked them away to have fun with elsewhere in the hospital.

All I wanted to do during that time was make people smile, but perhaps I pushed the boundaries a bit. Anyway, the staff were amazing. They had to put up with so much, and it can't be easy to watch all that pain and suffering. I can't thank them enough, but to be honest, I think they were probably itching to get rid of me, to ship me into rehab. And that's exactly what they did – just as soon as they'd fitted me with my first false leg.

The hi-tech machinery that allows me and other amputees to walk nowadays is a far cry from those early limbs I wore. Today I wear a leg that is constructed from carbon fibre and cushioned with shock absorbers; the foot is designed much like the blades or 'cheetah legs' that you sometimes see amputee athletes running on. These transfer the energy as you walk from the 'heel' to the 'toe'. The technology is amazing and progressing all the time. Thirty years ago things were very different. My first leg consisted of a leather corset round the thigh that I had to lace up, with a leather belt and a strap that went over my shoulder. There was a socket for my stump, and two metal bars riveted to the top were connected to a solid lump of wood that looked rather like a black banana with a flat bottom. It had nothing to reduce the impact of walking. They called it the Pylon, and I had basic machinery similar to that for almost a decade before the technology started to improve.

Walking on that leg was terribly painful, but it was better than not walking at all. I knew that I'd been given a second chance, and although my life could never follow the path that I had always intended, I knew I had to get on with things. To do as much with my life as I possibly could, to make up for all my friends and colleagues who had lost theirs. And I think it helped me come to understand something that few people do understand at such a young age: sometimes in life, you just have to count your blessings.

Chapter Six

Moving On

After eleven months at the Queen Elizabeth, I moved to RAF Chessington Hospital in Surrey. Now demolished, this installation was originally a balloon depot operated by RAF Balloon Command and was instrumental in Britain's defence against the Luftwaffe during the Second World War. By the time I arrived in 1980, it was one of two military rehab centres in the country, the other being the nearby former stately home Headley Court. Today Headley Court is a rehab centre for all wounded servicemen and women; back then it was only for those with the rank of sergeant and above. The 'grunts' went to Chessington. It was here that I would have to learn how to rebuild my life.

RAF Chessington was a pretty basic place. Its history as a balloon depot meant it was made up of cavernous hangars, with the patients billeted in somewhat rudimentary huts. But the standard of accommodation at

Chessington didn't matter, because the atmosphere there was fantastic.

The main aim of these rehab centres was to get those soldiers who had been less seriously injured than me back up to battle fitness. For those of us with more serious wounds, the aim was always to get us back to a state where we could be of some use to our regiments. So our days were highly structured. There was a muster parade and inspection each day, and we spent every morning and afternoon in the gym carrying out our exercise regimes, with physiotherapy classes interspersed throughout the week. The exercises were important, but it also felt good to be with a bunch of people who all had a single-minded determination to get better. And even though I was often still very restricted, because I had to use either a wheel-chair or crutches, being at Chessington gave me a certain amount of freedom, especially at the weekends.

When you've been so restricted for so long, you learn to value your freedom, to make the most of it. I was determined to do that, and so it was while I was in rehab at Chessington that I took my Army driving course. I came back to the Para depot at Aldershot and did a week-long course with a Polish driving instructor – an ex-airborne guy from the last war. We used a little black Mini with manual transmission, and he had a ruler that he'd flick my knuckles with every time I made a mistake. He did that to all his students, and I was glad to be treated the same as anyone else. Of course, the lack of feeling I had in my false leg made clutch control a bit of an issue.

It felt odd being at the Para depot, in front of all the
regimental top brass at RHQ, stuttering and starting out
of the main gate in the morning. But there was no way I
was going to let my disability hold me back. In the end it
was a great way to learn, and impossible not to pass your
test at the end of that intensive week of lessons. It was
such a high point for me to get my driving licence. It
meant mobility at the end of such a long period of
restriction.

With the money that the people of Nottingham had
raised for me, I bought my first car – a cobalt blue Ford
Capri – which seemed like a suitable way to spend the
money. That vehicle was so important to me that I can
still remember the registration number – WGH 538W.
And now, thirty years later, when I find it difficult to walk
because of the pain in my leg and I hate being in a wheelchair, my car is everything. That first car had automatic
transmission, so I could drive it even if I was unable to
wear my false leg for some reason. I still tend to favour
automatics for exactly that reason, though I do try to
drive manual cars whenever I can just so I can keep
practising.

There was no counselling in those days, and in truth I
didn't really feel the need for it, perhaps because I was just
so young and keen to get on with things, perhaps because
I knew I had the security of the Army all around me. I
tried just to enjoy the life that had so nearly been taken
away from me. I got out and about as much as I could, and
tried to socialize. On a Thursday evening they would put

on a disco, which members of the local community would come to. I met a few girls at these discos and had a couple of brief relationships, including one with one of the nurses. But nothing too serious – I was too young for that.

Any extra support that I needed came through the love and attention of my family. There was no financial support from the Army, so my family helped me out in that respect too. But, having been injured in Northern Ireland, I was eligible for a payment called Criminal Injuries Compensation. It was quite a substantial sum – enough, eventually, to buy the house in which I now live, and certainly enough to dispel any money worries for an 18-year-old.

During my time at Chessington I worked hard to get as fit as possible. I was obviously restricted in what exercises I could do, not only because of my leg but because of the damage to my hand. I also had to be careful with my grafted skin. Even now, although it is reasonably tough in places, I always have a sore or a bruise somewhere. Back then, though, it was like paper. The doctors had done as much for me as they possibly could by the time they discharged me to Chessington, but I was still fragile. If I so much as rubbed a fingernail across my skin, it would break; and I remember spending six weeks on the hospital ward at Chessington because my good foot had split and developed an abscess under the grafted skin. Once my wounds were fully healed, however, I was able to swim, and did so almost every day. With my bad leg, swimming was a bit more complicated than it had been before. I found that if I closed my eyes and swam 'normally', I'd just go round in a big circle. I soon learned how to compensate for the missing limb, however, to enable myself to swim in a straight line. And of course most of my propulsion came from my upper body. Even now, if I hold onto a float and kick, I simply won't go anywhere. But it was good for me, and in terms of cardiovascular exercise it made up for not being able to run around. In time I would become strong enough to train alongside the Army swimming teams. Aside from my sessions in the gym and the pool and my physiotherapy classes, the remainder of my days were devoted simply to putting weight back on. I was still very underweight and needed to pack in the calories as best I could.

During my time in hospital and rehab, I knew I had to get out and get going again. In order to do so I had to stay positive, but inevitably I was susceptible at times to dark thoughts and dark moods. Somebody had tried to kill me, after all; and they had succeeded in killing so many of my friends. I suppose I could have been forgiven for allowing my thoughts to turn to thoughts of revenge. And, to be honest, at times my mind did start to wander. Plans started to form. You get to know a lot of people as a soldier, people who go in different directions. Consequently, I had contacts that I knew would willingly hand me a list of those Provos who were thought to be responsible for the bombings, along with their home addresses. And with my military training I could quite easily have gone over to Ireland, tracked them down, and shot the lot.

I wonder how many people would have blamed me for doing so.

But thoughts of revenge and a positive mental attitude don't sit comfortably together. You can't be vengeful and constructive at the same time. And in any case I don't think I'm a naturally angry person. I had to teach myself to be philosophical about things. I knew what I'd signed up for when I joined the Army; I knew the risks I was taking. The job I had chosen had certain consequences. I had no love for the IRA, of course; but equally I had no wish for my life to be shadowed by carrying a grudge. Getting angry wouldn't do me any good, or help me heal. And being bitter and twisted takes up a lot of energy – energy that I decided would be much better directed towards getting better and getting on with my life.

So I did everything I could to put the memory of Warrenpoint behind me, to move on – even to the extent of not doing too much research into what happened that day. The first time I read a detailed account of that bank holiday Monday – apart from newspaper clippings at the time – was nearly thirty years later. While browsing in a bookshop I came across *Soldier*, the autobiography of General Sir Mike Jackson, Chief of the General Staff and the officer commanding B Company, 2 Para, in Northern Ireland at the time of the bombing. It was something of a body blow to open his book and see pictures of the four-tonner I'd been in that day, let alone to read his words and revisit that time which I had so carefully packed away in a box in my mind.

Some people call my attitude resilience. Some people call it bravery. It's neither of these things. It's just the way I am, and the way I've learned to cope.

Clearly, though, I couldn't entirely ignore what went on in Northern Ireland after the bombing. In 1998 large numbers of IRA members who had been convicted of atrocities were released from prison under the terms of the Good Friday Agreement. It angered a lot of people and I can understand why. No right-thinking person could be thrilled by the prospect of convicted murderers out and walking the streets, or by the idea of individuals with dubious histories serving in the House of Commons. Of course, these things make one take a deep breath. But, knowing that there was nothing I could do to help or hinder these events, I allowed myself to feel hopeful about them. Hopeful that it really did signal an end to the hostilities that had caused so much grief and suffering on both sides of the fence, and hopeful that those who had been released would use the opportunity to become better people and do something good with their lives.

Because now that my broken body was on the mend, that was exactly what I intended to do.

The problems people have are always relative to their own lives. Over the years, I've lost count of the number of people who have come up to me and said they wonder how I cope when their bad back or stiff shoulder seems to have such a profound effect on them. But I've discovered that what is important is not the injury itself, but how it changes your life. If someone's bad back is truly debilitating, that can be as bad an injury as mine.

The key, I decided early on, would be both to accept that my injuries had changed my life and also to realize that I had more reason than an able-bodied person to work out how I could achieve the best standard of living I possibly could. I used the loss of my friends and colleagues as a driving force. They were not *able* to enjoy their lives, so how could I even think about not making the most of mine? I had a duty to organize my life around my injury, rather than my injury around my life. It would be hard. I couldn't just go out and do ordinary things that people take for granted. I had to work out *how* to do them first, and how to manage my time so that I could get the most out of it. There was, and still is, only so much time I could spend on my feet in a single day before the pain caught up with me, so I needed to have a structured use of time and energy. I could think of it as making my life more difficult, or as making it more interesting. I decided on the latter.

At first I was embarrassed by my new leg. It wasn't so much that I had lost a limb that worried me. It was more that my prosthetic one *looked* so bad, like something from the First World War. Nowadays amputees routinely receive pretty space-age-looking limbs; back then my leg looked so old-fashioned, and was painted in such a gruesome supposedly 'flesh' colour, that for a long time I refused to wear shorts. Far easier to wear a pair of loose tracksuit bottoms than have something like that on display. It's human nature to stare at something a little bit different, but it doesn't take too many of the wrong kind of stares for an amputee to start feeling like a freak.

I felt like that for a good three or four years before something clicked inside of me. Why should *I* be embarrassed about the leg? I might be a little bit different from other people, but I certainly wasn't a freak. If other people wanted to be embarrassed about it, let them. I had no reason to be. It made life a lot more comfortable not having to wear shorts, and I even decided to make a feature of the prosthetic limb by painting it pillar-box red. I hope that any amputee reading this will understand, and perhaps be saved the months and years of embarrassment I suffered, time wasted staying inside because they're worried what people might think about them.

Embarrassment aside, my new leg, far from being a hindrance, was a revelation. I was bedridden, then stuck in a wheelchair, for so long that to be able to move about, albeit with pain and with less ease than before, was the most wonderful thing. I relished being able to stand up and look people in the eye, rather than gaze up at them from a chair. And it didn't matter if I was on crutches if now I could reach things that I couldn't reach before. I remember, when I was in hospital in Woolwich, my mum pushing me in my wheelchair down to the shops. A simple little excursion – just something to get me outside for a bit. Predictably, it wasn't as simple as it seemed. The wheelchairs we had back then were nothing like the hi-tech ones available today. Mum tried to get me down the kerb – in those days nobody thought to put ramps anywhere for disabled access – and the whole thing jammed. The traffic was whizzing by and one bandaged leg was sticking out. It was a nightmare for my poor mum. So, having a false leg, no matter how archaic it might have been, wasn't a setback. It opened doors and gave me the one thing I craved: independence.

That's not to say there weren't difficulties. I just had to keep my sense of humour. I was in Victoria shopping centre in Nottingham with my mum in the early days, wearing my Pylon leg, using crutches and standing on an escalator. All of a sudden, as I stepped off the escalator, one of the Pylon's metal bars snapped and the whole foot went off at a sideways angle. There was a Boots store just opposite, so with Mum's help I hobbled in and asked if they had anything I could patch myself up with. It was not, I imagine, a request they get very often. And the first time I bought shoes, the young lad who served me was more than a little shocked by the sight of my leg and foot.

From the moment I woke up in the Queen Elizabeth, through all the difficult time in hospital and the long period of rehabilitation, my main aim was always the same: to get back to the battalion. I never wanted to go home and lick my wounds. I wanted to get straight back to my other family: the Parachute Regiment. I had spent so long training to be a Para, and had set my heart on it from such an early age, that I wasn't going to let anything get in the way of my returning. The last thing I wanted was to be treated differently from everyone else. The regiment was brilliantly supportive, but you are of course limited as to what you can actually do in the Parachute Regiment if you're unable to run around. Front-line soldiering was clearly out of the question, so once I was discharged from RAF Chessington in 1981 I returned to 2 Para in Aldershot as part of the training wing of HQ Company – that section of the regiment that takes care of command and logistics.

I spent six months with HQ Company, trying to work out what to do with the rest of my life and find a role for myself. In truth I think I was working in the training wing because the regiment couldn't quite work out what to do with me. I did whatever little jobs needed doing, including a fair bit of driving now that I had my licence. I was asked, during my time with HQ Company, to go to Queensland in Australia. A man called Ken Bromley had set up a charity called Operation Good Samaritan. It was initially intended for those members of the Australian military who had been injured in Vietnam, but now he had opened it up to those who had suffered in the Northern Ireland conflict. The purpose of Operation Good Samaritan was simple: to give the recipients of Ken Bromley's generosity a bit of a break. We lounged around his house for six weeks – in a little cul-de-sac near the beach that could have been a set from *Neighbours* – got fed to death, and went on a few trips out. All in all it was a very pleasant and relaxing time – and a far cry from what I'd ever expected life in the Parachute Regiment to be like.

Back in the UK, my time at HQ Company passed quickly, and although I was glad to be back with the regiment, I felt frustrated at not having a definite role. So I was pleased when, at the end of six months, my boss, Barry Andrews, took me to one side. 'Paul,' he said, with a smile that suggested he'd just had a very good idea. 'Why don't you become a parachute rigger?'

I gave him a blank look. 'A parachute rigger?'

At that time my parachuting experience had been limited to the eight jumps I'd performed when earning my wings. I'd certainly never had an interest in – or even thought about – sport parachuting. The truth is that many guys in the regiment find the military side of parachute jumping so horrific that they'd never consider jumping out of a plane for fun. There was a precedent, however, for me to follow this path. A Para by the name of Albert Hooker had lost a leg in a motorcycle accident while serving in Bahrain. He'd gone on to work with the Red Devils just as they were starting up, and to become a qualified rigger for them. The similarity between Albert's injury and mine had clearly sparked an idea in Barry's mind.

In essence a parachute rigger is an engineer for parachutes. A good rigger is involved in anything and everything to do with them: from building a chute and its component parts from the raw materials, through servicing one that's on line, to modifying and repairing them. It might be the parachute jumpers who get all the glory, but not a single display jump, military jump or training jump can take place without the expertise of the riggers. In a sense, being a rigger is a bit like a desk job because there's so much sitting around as you stitch and prepare the chutes. That was why the officer commanding the training wing at HQ Company thought I would be ideally suited for it: I doubt he imagined where his suggestion would take me.

I was open-minded about what I wanted to do in the future, and Barry's suggestion sounded reasonable. So I went along to speak to Mick Munn, the team commander of the Red Devils, to find out if he would take me on as a trainee rigger. Mick was full of encouragement, but told me that unfortunately they were at full strength. He suggested I try the Joint Services Parachute Centre at Netheravon in Wiltshire.

I'd never heard of this place before, but soon found out that it's one of a number of Joint Services Adventure Training Centres situated all over the country – there's one specializing in sailing, for example, and another in diving – which play host to personnel from all across the armed forces. The Army is big on adventure training, as it brings out the right spirit in the guys and gives them a break from the demands of their front-line jobs. At Netheravon men from different units would take a two-week parachuting course, and it was staffed by people who all had a passionate interest in freefall jumping. All the junior staff were there for a year's training, during which time they hoped to rack up enough jumps to be able to return to their relevant regimental freefall display teams. The OC, Jerry O'Hara, was a member of the Parachute

Regiment, and so were the two sergeants in the rigging room, Jim and Jo, who had both been members of the Red Devils. The place was full of really focused, really professional guys, and I was immediately attracted to it.

Netheravon was also a bit more relaxed than the regular army environment. The rank structure dominates everything in the military, but among sportsmen – which is what everybody at Netheravon was – things were a bit more equal. It's not uncommon for a private to do a parachute jump with a general. In the regular army their paths would never cross.

I joined Netheravon as a trainee rigger. It wasn't what I *really* wanted to do, of course. I *wanted* to be a soldier, on the front line, fighting alongside my friends in the Falklands and elsewhere. But I'd grown accustomed to the idea that this was never going to happen, and although the business of parachute rigging could sometimes be a bit more sedentary and tedious than I really wanted, I was pleased to be doing something constructive. I embarked upon a two-year course that required 300 hours of recorded rigging work and a series of written exams. It was a stopgap, really, a way of doing something useful and keeping busy while I worked out what I actually wanted to do with my life. I was given a little cottage to live in – a Second World War mission hut, one of a line of them cut into the side of a hill on the airfield. They were very basic, but fine for my purposes.

Life was busy. Military guys would arrive for the two-week course, then there would be a civilian parachuting club at the weekend. It was an endless conveyor belt of new people to meet. The longer I was there, the more I learned and the more involved I became in the actual running of the parachute centre. But I didn't jump. I was an amputee, after all, and my good leg was weak and damaged.

It would be foolish to hurl myself out of an airplane, wouldn't it?

It started to become apparent that one of the biggest hurdles I was going to have to overcome was other people's perceptions of what I could and couldn't – or should and shouldn't – do. At Netheravon I bought myself an all-terrain trike – three wheels, big balloon tyres, a kind of predecessor to the quad bike, and very nippy. I used it to travel the half-mile from my accommodation to the hangar: too far for me to walk, but not far enough to make it worth starting the car up. At least, that was my excuse. The real reason for having the trike was that I just wanted one – the big airfield, plus the expanse of Salisbury Plain, were the perfect places to take it out. I was a young man with a hunger for excitement, and the trike went some way to providing it.

One weekend the wind got up and it was too blowy for parachuting, so I grabbed the opportunity to take the trike out for a spin around Salisbury Plain. I'd rigged it up with a thumb-throttle, a lever for the gears and autoclutch, along with a luggage rack at the back which meant

I could leave my leg at home but take my crutches with me. Like most bikes, the trike had a reserve fuel tank. If you run out of petrol, you switch to your reserve and that should be enough to get you home. At least that's the theory. I wouldn't say I exactly had a habit of forgetting that I was running the bike on reserve, but that's what I did this day! I was bombing round the dirt tracks, doing wheelies, kicking up clouds of dust, and generally having an excellent time, when I heard the tell-tale phut-phut of the engine dying on me.

I looked around. All I could see was the expanse of Salisbury Plain for miles around. In those days before mobile phones, I was stuck. Without my leg. Miles from anywhere. There weren't many options. I could leave the trike there and try to hop back, or do what I could to push it. I didn't really want to leave it by itself, so I decided on the second option. I got off, leant over the rack at the back, held the handlebars, and started push-ing with one foot – not the easiest manoeuvre in the world.

I'd managed to cover a mile or so when I heard a famil-iar noise: a helicopter flying nearby. Nothing new there: the airspace above Salisbury Plain was always full of choppers. But as I carried on pushing I realized that the noise was getting louder and louder. Out of the corner of my eye I noticed a shadow. I looked round to see a helicopter at a safe distance of about forty feet, and hovering four or five feet above the ground. And not just any helicopter – a massive black Chinook with its distinctive double rotary blade. I could see the pilots looking at me – unsurprisingly, as I must have been a rather unusual sight.

I wasn't quite sure how to react. Should I just ignore them? Should I wave? In the end I thought it would be funny to put my thumb out, as though hitching a lift. I fully expected the pilots to have a laugh and fly away.

That's not what happened at all. The Chinook flew around in front of me and landed. I watched in astonishment as the enormous tailgate slowly lowered to reveal the aircraft's loadmaster, helmet on and intercom cable in hand. He ran out of the chopper towards me.

'*Hey, man!*' he yelled in an American accent. '*What you doing? What's wrong?*'

I explained that I'd run out of petrol.

'*Where you going?*'

'Er, just to the airfield at Netheravon.'

'*Hold on!*'

The loadie ran back up the tailgate and got on his radio to the pilot, before running back out again.

'*Hey, we'll take you, man!*'

He helped me push the bike up the tailgate and into the belly of the enormous helicopter. Moments later the tailgate hissed shut and we rose up over Salisbury Plain and flew back to the air base. It was my first time in one of these amazing aircraft.

We touched down at the parachute centre end of Netheravon. Now, parachute centres can be rather bleak places when the weather's not right for jumping.

Everyone was moping round feeling peeved that they couldn't jump. So the sudden, unexpected arrival of an American Chinook was quite an event. Everyone from the centre congregated outside to watch it land, and I knew what they were all thinking. It's in a parachute enthusiast's DNA, when they see a new aircraft, to wonder what it would be like to jump out of it. Chinooks are famously great aircraft to jump from: you can fit loads of people inside, walk to the edge of the ramp, and dive off. As the loadie and I pushed the bike off the back of the chopper, everyone from the parachute centre started flooding towards us.

I sheepishly explained what had happened on Salisbury Plain, but the guys were more interested in chatting up the Chinook crew. The Americans were over in the UK on training exercises, and had just been flying around to make up their flying hours. It meant they had nowhere special to be, so next thing I knew, every man and his dog were getting their parachute gear on and – despite the bad winds – piling into the Chinook. The Americans took them all up and gave them a freebie jump. The chopper was full to capacity, so there must have been about fifty people in it. Of all of them, only about two hit the drop zone at Netheravon; the remainder were scattered all over the countryside by the wind, but they were more than happy to drag their chutes back to the DZ after the thrill of the jump, and for months afterwards they reminisced about the time the man with one leg hitched a lift on a Chinook.

As for me, I stood at the DZ watching it disappear into the air, and wondering if it would really have been so ridiculous for an amputee to join them.

Chapter Seven

A Leap of Faith

My desire for a bit of excitement didn't stop at riding motorbikes. What I really wanted to do, rather than just rigging parachutes, was to use one. The more time I spent at Netheravon, the more I wanted that chance. I was forced to watch from the sidelines as my colleagues jumped out of planes, desperate to join in the thrill all the other guys were experiencing. Part of me felt like a child excluded from the other kids' games. All I wanted to do was to be allowed to join in.

Whenever I suggested it to the Netheravon staff, I always met with the same reply: a sturdy no. I suppose that if I look at it from their point of view, it wasn't an unreasonable response. I was an amputee, and half the time I had to get around on crutches. Sport parachuting was very much in its infancy back then, and all student jumping was done using round parachutes, as opposed to the square parachutes you're likely to see nowadays. The problem with round parachutes, as I knew from my parachute training with the regiment, was that the landings could be pretty heavy, and this could be problematic with my injuries. A motorbike was one thing, but throwing myself out of an airplane? They thought I might kill myself, and nobody was willing to let me take the risk. I was allowed as many trips as I wanted in the centre's Britten-Norman Islander aircraft as it flew up to altitude above the drop zone – I even became quite adept at flying it, as the pilots used to allow me to take the controls on the way back down. But as far as the team at Netheravon were concerned, it was fine for me to land the plane, but I was to stay well and truly *in* it. That was the sensible, safe thing to do.

I didn't see it that way. For me it was like a red rag to a bull. When everybody else is doing something you want to do, and you're told you can't, it makes you more driven. From my perspective, the lack of a leg was no obstacle at all. So I kept banging on at them. Not 'Can I jump?' but '*When* can I jump?' It's the squeaky hinge that gets the grease, and I figured that if I was persistent enough, they'd give in sooner or later.

I was right. Sort of. After nearly a year of pestering, I was allowed to do a water jump. This would be fine, I argued: my legs would be no problem in the air, and a water landing would be much softer than one on land.

The plan was to fly over Studland Bay, near Poole in Dorset, and our DZ would be the sea. As the time to jump grew nearer, however, my confidence started to waver. It's all very well being eager to jump when you're safely on the ground; it's a different matter when the aircraft lifts off. For that first jump I was, not to put too fine a point on it, bricking myself. A lot had happened since my training with the regiment, so I was worried I might not still have the skills or the love of jumping, and had a nagging doubt that I might have made a terrible decision. Landing in the drink is not without its risks. If your parachute collapses on top of you and you're in the water, you risk drowning, so you have to cut the chute away before you land. It's a lot to remember, especially for an inexperienced amputee.

Skydiving with one leg was something nobody else had ever done in the UK. I was breaking new ground, but would I end up breaking myself? But I couldn't say anything – I had, after all, been plaguing the staff at Netheravon for a long time, and I wasn't going to back out now. And anyway this was something I *had* to do. For me. For other amputees. For the guys who lost their lives at Warrenpoint.

The parachute centre used to organize a water jump for senior officers each year – it's a bit safer to throw a briga-dier out of a plane and into the water than onto land – and for my first jump I joined one of these groups. So I found myself in a plane with General Sir John Stanier, Brigadier Walker, Major Jerry O'Hara and the then Major Mike Gray, who would later become Commandant General of the Parachute Regiment and be awarded France's Légion d'honneur. But as I said, sport is a great leveller.

Just getting to the plane was a challenge. I was wearing a life jacket and carrying two parachutes – a main chute and a reserve – while hobbling across the tarmac with just one leg and a pair of crutches. It was painful, and an unwelcome reminder of why this jump was such a big deal. There was no turning back, though. Now it really did feel as if the whole world was watching – *my* whole world anyway. My family had come down to see me jump, and all my friends from the parachute centre were willing me on. I gritted my teeth and tried to forget about the pain as I hobbled towards the aircraft.

Inside the plane, I tried to draw attention away from the discomfort I was experiencing by putting on my stump puppet. Quite what the top brass thought of me and Arfur, I don't know, but soon the wheels were off the ground and we were climbing to our jumping height of 3,500 feet.

All sorts of things go through your head in the moments before a parachute jump. You sit at the exit of the plane, attached to the static-line cable, your ears filled with the roar of the wind as you prepare to push yourself out and put your body in a position that will enable you to fall stable. I worried about what would happen when I hit the water, and I felt awkward surrounded by all these high-ranking officers. It was a sensory overload – one that could only be relieved the moment I fell from the plane.

And what a moment it was!

To describe that first jump is to describe freedom. After the initial rush of freefall, the static line kicked in and my parachute billowed out above my body. For me that moment was an epiphany. I experienced the usual thrill that captivates most people when they jump, of course. But there was so much more than that. Ever since Warrenpoint I'd been shackled by pain. It was my constant companion, whenever I put pressure on my leg. It had accompanied me right up to the airplane. But in the air, as I drifted down into Studland Bay, there was no pressure. And that meant no pain. For that short time I was free: free to fall, and free of pain. A little moment of bliss and, for the first time since I'd been blown up, I was on a level playing field with other people.

For those short few minutes, I was normal once again.

When I came back down to earth, the sense of achievement was immense. I'd proved that I could do it, and now all I wanted was to do it again. I performed eight water jumps in all during my time at Netheravon, each one more fantastic than the last as my eyes were opened up to the freedom of parachuting. With each jump I grew increasingly in love with the sport, with the sensation and the freedom and the lack of pain. So much so that, before long, water jumps weren't enough. I wanted the real thing, but it still seemed impossible. Hitting land was a different ball game from hitting water, and nothing was going to change the state of my legs. Maybe I was just going to have to get used to the idea that this was something I could never achieve.

* * *

In September 1982 I was sent to Cyprus for a couple of months – my first posting of many – to the Joint Services Adventure Training Centre in Dhekelia. Located in the British Eastern Sovereign Base area, the centre was a bit like a small Netheravon in the sun. It was there primarily to provide outdoor activities for the British troops stationed on the island, but it also played host to visiting troops and UN forces, who would go there to take courses in sub-aqua diving, off-shore sailing, kayaking, canoeing and climbing, as well as parachuting, with the aim of helping their morale, fitness, and team-working abilities. The parachute centre was run by one man, with three staff on loan and a small Cessna 182 aircraft. It was a thrill to be able to go – I'd never been to Cyprus before and the climate there was a lot more clement than the wilds of Salisbury Plain – and I managed to do a few jumps into the waters of the Mediterranean. I went back to Netheravon at the end of 1982, eager to return to that beautiful island.

By this time I was keener than ever before to try a proper land jump, but the people at Netheravon were as reluctant as ever. Until, that is, I'd been there for a couple of years. A vague acquaintance of mine called John Ricks – a former Red Devil, who had recently gone to work for a commercial parachute company named GQ Parachutes – approached me. 'Paul,' he said. 'Have a look at this.'

'What is it?'

He smiled. 'A new kind of parachute.'

The chute John gave me had been designed specifically for the special forces, and it was very similar to the one they still use today. Back then, in the early 1980s, most student parachute jumping was done using a round parachute – the kind I'd trained on and was now using for my water jumps. These chutes have certain limitations. For one thing, they're not very manoeuvrable. It is possible to predict where a round parachute will land, but to do this involves extra reliance on the preparation that is done at the beginning of each day of jumping. The aircraft will fly over the drop zone – which will be a wide, flat, open space without any obstacles – at the same height at which the parachute would normally open, about 2,500 feet. When the plane is over the centre of the DZ, the jumpmaster will throw out a wind-drift indicator. This is a weighted streamer of paper that is designed to fall at the same rate as a person under a parachute. By establishing where the indicator lands, you can work out what wind forces will be at play, and adjust the location at which you jump from the aircraft accordingly.

The lack of manoeuvrability of a round parachute was something I could deal with. The problem was the nature of the landing. Round parachutes tend to bring you back down to earth with quite a bump, and that was why, during my para training, we had spent so long practising our landings before we even went near an aircraft. This heavy landing was the main reason why I wasn't allowed to do a land jump.

However, the nature of special-forces soldiering is such that a higher degree of precision is beneficial, as is a large canopy that can support more weight. Often, when units such as the SAS are inserted into a combat zone by parachute, their aircraft fly very high along commercial airline routes. This avoids suspicion, and because the jumper will reach terminal velocity – the highest speed at which a body can fall – and continue at this rate until very close to the ground, they are less likely to cause any splash on radar, making for a stealthier insertion. This is called a HALO jump – High Altitude, Low Opening. Alternatively they might perform a HAHO jump – High Altitude, High Opening – which allows them to be inserted from the plane in one location and fly, possibly over borders, to another. Because all this takes place from such a high altitude, the jumper needs to carry an oxygen canister, and in a military scenario they will most likely be carrying quite a lot of personal equipment – possibly twice their body weight. With a more manoeuvrable parachute – one that can effectively be flown by the user – they can insert themselves into specific coordinates even when dropped from a very great height. Modern square parachutes can move forwards at a rate of 40-odd mph, and the larger canopy means they can safely carry more weight.

There was no way I was going to be doing any special-forces soldiering, but that didn't mean I couldn't take advantage of their technology. This new parachute was square rather than round, and had a much larger canopy of 360 square feet. (Over time, as my abilities and the technology advanced, I would be able to reduce the size of this canopy.) As a consequence of this different shape and size, it's possible to land much more slowly, and therefore lightly. With one of these parachutes you can more or less tiptoe back down to earth. And for my purposes, that would obviously be a great benefit. The chute that John Ricks lent me was just a demonstration model, so it wasn't camouflaged in the way that a special-forces chute would be, but in other respects it was identical. And while it wasn't suitable for static-line jumping, as an accomplished rigger I could modify it so it was.

There was a drawback. Being twice as large as a regular parachute, it was twice as heavy. This would make it difficult to get to the aircraft, because my false leg made carrying heavy weights a bit of a chore. But I wasn't going to let that hold me back. This new parachute was a revelation. As it afforded a softer landing, it meant I got the thumbs-up from the Netheravon staff. And so it was that I was allowed to do my first land jump – something I would never have really thought possible with mangled legs like mine. It was an immensely proud moment, and now that I'd shown I could do it, I was able to work my way up through the British Parachute Association's category system. This was the first time anyone had done this on a square canopy.

The category system is broken down into eight separate grades, each one a little more complicated than the last. Category 1 requires that the jumper has undergone at least six hours' ground training and been given the all-clear to make a first static-line jump. If the jumper can show that they are able to fall stable and count for the duration of their fall, they achieve Category 2. For Category 3 you need to perform three consecutive dummy ripcord pulls – this means you are jumping from a static line but practising the technique of opening your own chute. To achieve Category 4 you need to demonstrate the ability to move from static-line jumps to delayed-opening jumps, where you activate the parachute between three and five seconds after leaving the aircraft. For Category 5 you do the same thing, but release the chute after about ten seconds of freefall; and for Category 6 after about fifteen seconds, and with the use of an altimeter. Now you have enough time in freefall to carry out certain manoeuvres in the air. Category 7 requires you to show that you can perform controlled 360-degree turns in either direction. Category 8 is where the fun starts: you must perform an unstable exit by pulling your knees up to your chest as you leave the aircraft, a dive exit, and back loops. Once you've moved through the category system, you can proceed to becoming a jumpmaster and then start formation skydiving.

All the training I'd done with the Parachute Regiment had involved automatic static-line jumping, as had my water jumps in Netheravon and Cyprus. I threw myself into moving up the scale of the category system, however, and made good progress, although my legs did hinder things a little between Categories 4 and 5. When I went for the ten-second delay, I found my body was turning because my leg was missing, but I didn't have enough time to work out what I was supposed to do and so couldn't get into a position where I was falling steady, so I kept being put back onto a five-second delay. Each time I tried to move up to ten seconds, I failed, and was put back to the five-second delay. It felt like an impassable barrier, and my dream of becoming a fully qualified skydiver might have stopped there had a guy called Bob Charters not come to the parachute centre. He put me straight onto a twenty-second delay, which gave me sufficient time to correct my position to fall without turning. It meant I could now move on and complete the course.

The big goal of the category system is to get you to a level where you are able to go off and skydive on your own, without having to be watched and critiqued at every jump. For me it was another form of freedom. It was fantastic to learn how to freefall, and how to move around in the air; even more than that, it felt like a real achievement to do all this given the state of my body.

Under canopy, as I'd already found out, I was able to be active and yet pain-free. In freefall there were other advantages. Ever since I'd woken up in that hospital bed after Warrenpoint, my mobility had been restricted. I'd tried not to let it hold me back, of course, but the reality was that I couldn't move around like other people. When you're skydiving, however, you're effectively flying your body. You don't tumble out of control, but rather you move and slide around the sky. Once I'd got used to doing this, taking into account my lack of symmetry, I soon found that I could be the equal of any other skydiver in the world, if I just put my mind to it. Lack of mobility wasn't a problem. For the first time in years, I wasn't hindered by my injuries.

It was another shackle cast away. Another form of freedom. But this wasn't just the freedom to drift down to earth without pain. It was so much more than that. I could go from a position of limited mobility to one of almost infinite mobility. On the ground I could only move around with pain and difficulty. In the air, I could fly. Ever since Warrenpoint I'd been technically disabled. But I didn't want people to *think* of me as being disabled. I wanted, as far as was possible, to do whatever able-bodied people could do. To push the boundaries. Now, at least in the field of parachuting, I was able to do that.

There's a couple of guys I know called Al and Swifty. Both had lost both legs to bombs in Northern Ireland and were confined to a wheelchair, apart from when they attached short, stumpy legs they'd had made for canoeing. As happens so often with people who sustain such terrible injuries, their lives started to grow devoid of direction. They just didn't know what to do with themselves. I introduced them to skydiving with a tandem jump and now it's Al's whole life. He's married to a skydiver; he teaches skydiving; and he spends every moment of his free time in the air. Swifty got to a very high standard, but has now moved on to new adventures.

It's a source of immense pride for me to know that none of what Al and Swifty have achieved would have been possible had I not – literally – taken the plunge and started skydiving. It would have been the easiest thing in the world to submit to my injuries, and I'm sure nobody would have blamed me for sitting behind a desk for the rest of my Army career.

But sometimes the easy path isn't the right path to take. When I lost my leg the perception of what disabled men and women could and couldn't do was set in stone. My determination to jump from an aircraft might seem like a small thing, but it chipped a few chunks away from that stone and in so doing it changed not only my life, but other people's. It's hugely satisfying to me that I paved the way for Al and Swifty – and other amputees – to start skydiving, and to know that I've changed not only the system, but also the general perception about what so-called disabled people can and can't do. I know that it has improved people's lives. And even if I never achieved anything else, that would be enough.

Years previously I had made myself a promise that I was going to live my life to the very full in memory of those who'd had their lives taken away at Warrenpoint. I certainly felt like I was fulfilling that promise.

Chapter Eight

Red Devil

In 1983 my brother John passed away. It was a great blow for our family, and for my mum in particular. She had lost a husband and a son; her other son had sustained terrible injuries. There must have been times when she wondered how much more the world could throw at her. John was a good deal older than me, but I missed him terribly. He was like a brother, an uncle and a mentor all rolled into one, and my world was immeasurably poorer without him. I miss him to this day.

But life had to continue. When I was working at Netheravon we would sometimes head into Salisbury to see a film or hang out in a few of the pubs. There was one place we'd go to quite often for a drink, and it was here that I met Sheila. She was working temporarily as a barmaid while she waited to start her nursing training, and as time passed we became friendly. It's not always very easy for someone who is disabled to get close to an able-bodied person, but Sheila was lovely. Slim, blonde, down-to-earth and laid-back, she was the sort of woman I felt I could chat to for ever.

Christmas of 1983 approached, and a party was planned at the parachute centre – a posh shirt-and-tie do where everyone was allowed to bring a partner. I didn't have anyone I could bring, so I asked Sheila. She agreed, and things blossomed from there. We started seeing each other on a more regular basis, and soon we were an item.

Now that I had Sheila and my jumping, I began to feel that the sky was – quite literally – the limit. Back in the 1980s, anybody who started jumping seriously within the military had a particular aim, and that was to join their regiment's freefall display team. There were several display teams, including those from the Royal Green Jackets, the Light Infantry, the Queen's, and the Marines. A lot of these freefall display teams no longer exist because of cutbacks to the Army, but the most famous one, then as now, was the freefall display team of the Parachute Regiment, the Red Devils.

Almost by default, I found myself drawn onto the path that might eventually lead to being considered for the Red Devils. I knew it was a big ask for an amputee to join such an illustrious skydiving team, but I was inspired by others I'd heard of. In America there was an outfit called Pieces of Eight, which comprised eight amputees performing eight-way skydives; and Captain Hook and the Sky Pirates were led by an amputee who jumped wearing a hook instead of a hand. If they could do it, why not me?

The standard of skydiving needed to join the Red Devils was incredibly high. You needed to have completed a minimum of 250 jumps and to have achieved a very high level of technical competence so as to avoid the many things that can go wrong during display parachuting. If I was to reach that level, I was going to have to work very hard. Fortunately I had the opportunity to do so.

In February 1984 I was posted once more to the parachute centre in Cyprus, this time for a stay of nearly two years. Ostensibly my role there was as a parachute rigger, but because it was such a small centre I ended up doing a bit of everything, including refuelling the aircraft and handling the manifesting – recording the details of all the flights made and jumps taken. I learned a hell of a lot during that time, but best of all I had the opportunity to jump every day. It was the best way to progress. Skydiving is addictive, like a computer game: each time you play you want to go back and improve your score just a little bit. Lots of people can't do that, because it's an expensive pastime; but I was able to build on my skills every day.

It was great to be back in Cyprus. I loved my time at the parachute centre and in the air. But there was something missing. For my first couple of months I corresponded regularly with Sheila, but my being away made us both realize how much we wanted to be with each other. At Easter that first year I was given some leave, so I returned home, and the first thing I did was ask Sheila to marry me.

It was a very rushed wedding: a flurry of arrange-
ments followed by a ceremony two weeks later. With
hindsight, it feels as if it all happened very suddenly –
perhaps too suddenly. But at the time it absolutely seemed
like the sensible thing to do. Cyprus can be a lonely place
in the winter, and although I was doing everything I
could not to let my injury get in the way of my life, deep
down I suppose I must have felt certain insecurities about
the future – about how likely I was to find somebody willing to settle down with someone whose body had been
damaged as badly as mine. Looking back, I think that my
desire to settle down was a direct consequence of my
accident. But all I remember feeling at the time is happi-
ness that Sheila wanted to be with me. When I returned
to Cyprus at the end of my leave, I was a married man.
Sheila didn't join me immediately. First I had to arrange
army quarters for us, but a month later she flew out to
join me, and finally we were able to be together.

My work continued much as before. I took advantage
of all the activities at the centre – diving, canoeing, and
gliding – and carried on as a rigger, all the while getting
my jump numbers up. I still had hopes of joining the freefall team, after all. While I was there I started working
towards a diving qualification. My eardrums had burst at
Warrenpoint and, although they had been grafted in
hospital, I couldn't go terribly deep, but I was able to
work towards the British Sub Aqua Club diving qualification. To gain this, I had to be able to tread water for three
minutes with my hands above my head – easy with two

legs, very difficult when you've only got one. Half the time I had my head under the water, just holding my breath while I gathered the strength to push myself up and gulp in some more air. Once I'd got my BSAC qualification, I did a mile-long swim underwater to raise money for charity. I also got my motorbike licence while I was in Cyprus, but I kept that a secret from my mum to save her worries.

Our first son, Ben, was born just over a year after Sheila and I married, in October 1985. A month later my tour of Cyprus came to an end, so our little family headed back to England. I think both Sheila and I would have liked to stay on a bit longer, but there were good reasons for coming back. First and foremost, in the Army you do what you're told. But the big draw was that a place was available in the Red Devils. Now that I'd got sufficient jumps under my belt, they were receptive to the idea of my joining the team, despite my injuries. It was too good an opportunity to pass up.

The Red Devils freefall team is maintained as a recruiting device for the Army in general and the Parachute Regiment in particular. It's very successful in this respect. When I joined, it had been in existence for just over twenty years. By 1963 sport parachuting had a small but enthusiastic following, with a recognized controlling body in the British Parachuting Association. And although, back in the early 1960s, British parachuting teams were some way from being the best in the world, they weren't bad. Parachute displays were uncommon but increasing in popularity and, perhaps unsurprisingly, many of the para-chuting enthusiasts came from the armed forces. There was a successful team of RAF parachute jump instructors based at No. 1 Parachute Training School, where fifteen years later I would train to get my wings. But the most accomplished jumpers were those from 22 SAS. The Brit-ish team for the 1962 World Parachute Championships all came from the SAS, though over time this regiment would become less involved in sport jumping because of its commitments elsewhere.

As far as the Parachute Regiment was concerned, 1, 2 and 3 Para all had a separate club, and a number of other different clubs were being formed by other units, includ-ing a successful one started by the Royal Green Jackets. As a result of all this embryonic activity, the Army Para-chute Association came into being. The APA's first aircraft, a de Havilland Rapide, was donated by the cigar-ette company Rothmans – not something that would happen nowadays, I think.

On 1 January 1964 Lieutenant Edward Gardener found himself at Para HQ, in charge of the first military para-chute freefall display team, the Red Devils. The team was nothing like as well equipped as it is today; more alarm-ingly, it didn't even contain very many well-trained jump-ers. The regiment was about to be deployed to Bahrain, so it was understandably reluctant to release all its most experienced parachutists to the Red Devils. The three battalions of Paras allowed a combined total of thirteen men to join the team. Of these, the contingent from 2 Para, my battalion, was by far the least experienced, some of them having completed only between ten and twenty jumps. It was a far cry from the 250 that are required today, and there was a lot of work to be done with them. The Red Devils were invited by the Golden Knights – the US Army Parachute Team – to visit them at Fort Bragg in North Carolina for a few weeks' training. Unfortunately the invitation was rescinded when the CIA discovered a shipment of British Leyland buses being sent, with the blessing of the British government, to Cuba, sparking an awkward diplomatic moment between the UK and the United States.

As the Red Devils had next to no funds, they were unable to hire the Army Parachute Association's Rapide aircraft, or any other civilian aircraft. They weren't even able to supply parachutes to the team. So the guys in the team not only had to buy their own equipment, but also pay for their own training jumps. A big ask, given that this was for an official duty, part of their job. But enthusiasm is part of the Paras' mentality, and it seems they did all this willingly enough.

After a few months Lieutenant Gardener had ensured that his fledgeling Red Devils had all performed at least fifty jumps. But this was far from ideal in terms of experience, so their first parachute displays involved only very simple routines – little more than mass exits from the aircraft with smoke attached to the heels of some of the men. Given their relative lack of experience, it was enough to get all the men down safely in the target area of the drop zone.

In the first year of their existence the Red Devils performed thirty display jumps. They were all completed without injury, but not without incident. One poor chap missed the DZ and ended up inside a locked tennis court. But as time passed they became increasingly skilled. On 7 April 1965 they jumped, along with the Golden Knights – relations between the two countries having thawed by now – at the opening of the Paras' Montgomery Lines barracks in Aldershot. It was, at the time, the biggest skydiving event ever to take place in Britain, and the Red Devils were well on their way to becoming the major force in freefall jumping that they were when I came on the scene.

They remain a unique organization. Members of the team put their military career on hold and are there on detachment from the regiment. And in the same way that the Parachute Regiment itself draws a certain type of person into its ranks, so the freefall team is made up of an exceptional group of guys. Everyone is single-mindedly focused on the sport, and on being the best they can possibly be. At any one time there are only about twenty-five people on the team, each one staying for a couple of years, though as I write this the regiment needs all the manpower it can get for its forthcoming tour in Afghanistan, so there is only a skeleton team. This means that there have only been about 400 Red Devils in the team's history. There is a definite sense among them that they are part of an elite band.

Sport parachuting has evolved very quickly since the early days of the Red Devils. New chutes, new disciplines, and new techniques have been developed, and the Paras' freefall team have been at the forefront of that evolution ever since their inception; indeed much of it can be attributed to the Red Devils themselves.

The purpose of the Red Devils is to perform parachute displays. It's got to be the best way of jumping. An actor without an audience is no good; similarly, a freefall jumper gets a lot back from performing in front of thousands of people. There's an excitement that comes from knowing how much they are marvelling at you doing what you love, and also from travelling to different places around the country and jumping in different conditions. Your drop zone might be a football pitch or a stadium, or surrounded by mountains. And there are no dummy runs – you have to work out your approach as you're flying, and deal with the wind currents as well as performing your complicated aeronautical stunts.

Joining the Red Devils is a big moment for everyone. But I think perhaps it meant as much to me as to anyone. There are milestones in my life that make me proud: earning my red beret and my wings; my first parachute jumps onto water and land. But being accepted into the Red Devils is as important as any of these. Based back in Aldershot, I was surrounded by two battalions of my regiment, 1 and 2 Para, which meant a lot of familiar faces and a feeling of being back in the heart of my second family – something that perhaps only those who have served with the airborne forces could ever fully understand. I could never forget the desperation I experienced, after being blown up, at the thought that I might never be able to play an active role within the battalion again. But now I was back within the airborne community, obliged to wear a uniform once again, and just so happy to be part of it. I'd managed to negotiate a path back into the regiment, not as a hanger-on, placed into some administrative position because nobody knew what else to do with me, but as a proper, active member.

I'd worked my way up to being an advanced parachute rigger – something I'd initially intended to do only while I worked out what I wanted to do with my life – and then gone on to become an experienced freefall jumper. I had what I considered to be a real job for the first time since Warrenpoint – a job of my own choosing, and one that I'd had to work hard towards. I knew I could never be a soldier again, but that didn't mean I couldn't play my part. The arrival of an amputee on the freefall team caused a certain amount of national publicity, especially as at the time I was still the only skydiving amputee in the country. But I tried not to push that side of things, because I didn't want to be singled out for this reason. I just wanted to get on with things and be treated like any other able-bodied guy. The team certainly did that: I never got the impression that they thought of me as anything other than one of the lads, and I was pleased that I was never used for publicity, which would have made me most uncomfortable (although occasionally the commentator on displays would build me up a bit).

When you first join the team, you go through a period that is a bit like an apprenticeship. The Red Devils have training camps, not only in the UK but also abroad, where they all go to train together so that the old hands can keep their skills up and the new boys can learn all about display jumping. And I had plenty to learn. My basic skills were good and I was able to show that I had mastered the most important skill of parachuting, and that is landing safely where you want to land. It doesn't matter what kind of aeronautical pyrotechnics you manage to achieve; if you can't stop yourself drifting off above buildings or roads, or into the crowd at a display, you're a danger not only to yourself but also to people on the ground. When a bunch of guys jump out of an airplane there's an element of human error involved: jump a bit too early, or a bit too late, and you can find yourself a long way from the drop zone. When you're descending at 180 mph in a head-down tracking position, you have to think fast if this happens, and scan the land below for a suitable place. This happened to me once over Aldershot, and I ended up landing in a school playing field. It was a nice wide space, but still hazardous because you had to be aware of any kids on the ground – although those who saw it did enjoy their own little parachute display. Other guys have had to land accurately on quiet roads in circumstances like this. In short, your landing skills need to be excellent.

You also need to be able to stay level-headed in the event that your canopy doesn't open properly. This only ever happened to me three times: one of those times was just a freak of nature, when the deployment system put a knot in itself; the other two times were a result, I think, of me rush-packing. Everyone is well drilled for events such as this. You must cut away the main chute, go back into freefall, and engage your much simpler reserve chute – and hope that everything's OK with that one.

Now I was a Red Devil, however, I also had to improve the technique of flying my body in the air so that I would be better at physically joining up with other members of the team. The principles are similar to those involved in scuba-diving. If you keep your body in a stable position, you'll just fall downwards under the force of gravity. If you put your arms forward and 'grab' more air, you'll slide backwards; put your legs out and you'll go forwards. As I'd found with swimming, this involved a bit of weight compensation because my false leg makes me rather asymmetrical, but I soon got the hang of it and after a while I didn't even have to think about it.

Once I'd learned how to fly, I had to learn the principles of 'relative work'. This involves formation flying, where the team joins up in mid-air to create various shapes, and often does a number of different formations during a single jump. And then there was 'canopy relative work', or CRW, which is the same thing but using parachutes. While this is visually spectacular, it's potentially dangerous. It can, for example, involve stacks of several men, their feet just above each other's shoulders and their canopies touching. If the lines or canopies get tangled – and this does sometimes happen – the canopies can deflate and wrap around the jumpers, and so are rendered useless. In such a situation each man needs to disengage from the formation in a particular order, and each of them may need to use the sharp knife he carries to cut away the main canopy, before activating his reserve chute to get him back down to earth. But assuming everything went according to plan, we would always separate, or engage our chutes if it was principally a freefall display, at a prearranged height – sometimes just before landing. This would be marked by the altimeters that we all wore on our wrist. Nowadays, for safety purposes, we have mechanisms that open the reserve parachute at a given altitude if for some reason we get knocked unconscious in the air and are unable to operate it ourselves, but back in the 1980s we didn't have such technology.

Before long I was able to start display work. We jumped at all sorts of events and places, from Army passing-out parades to county shows to football grounds, with smoke bombs attached to our ankles to make the whole thing look more impressive from down below. Most of these events take place during the summer, when the weather is more suitable, and at weekends, because more people can come along. A typical display might involve four initial jumpers, with smoke, in a star formation. Then, two diamond trackers might fly, head down and arms tight by their sides, away from the star, counting twenty seconds before turning and flying back towards each other, smoke trailing behind them all the way. While this is happening, more team members might leave the aircraft and open their chutes immediately, stacking them up in different formations. Or, for lower-altitude displays, we might do a 'team stack', where the team leaves the aircraft one after the other, all watching the first to leave. When he opens his chute the rest of the team do the same in unison, then fly with their canopies close together, one above the other. Simple when you know how!

Of all the jumps that stick in my mind, the most prestigious was when we jumped for the Queen at the Joint Services Defence College – a training academy by the river in Greenwich which was subsequently amalgamated into the Joint Services Command and Staff College. Her Majesty was there to inspect the college and its personnel, and as part of the proceedings the Red Devils were to put in an appearance.

It was a difficult jump with a small drop zone – the river on one side and three-storey buildings on three other sides. Jumping in London is a bit more difficult than elsewhere because the air traffic coming into Heathrow means you're only allowed to jump from 1,200 feet. We started out from the barracks in Aldershot, where two Chinooks – the impressive double-bladed support choppers that are currently so indispensable in Afghanistan – picked us up. One of them was for us, one of them was for back-up, just in case the first broke down. This was an extravagance that even the Red Devils weren't normally afforded. Nobody wanted to take any chances during a display for Her Majesty!

Twenty-five of us jumped from just north of the Thames, opening our parachutes immediately as we got our first view of the DZ, before flying over the river and coming in to land on the southern bank. Our normal landing routine was very military: we would all land on one knee and wait for everyone else to hit the ground while removing our parachutes and putting on our red berets. The highest-ranked member of the team would then give a nod to indicate that we should all march in a regimented line and come to attention, at which point the organizer of the event, or whichever guest of honour or dignitary happened to be present, would come and talk to us and shake our hands.

On this occasion things were a bit different. The moment we landed, some official ushered us off round the corner, the intention clearly being that we should keep our distance from the royal party. We'd done our bit – now it was time to clear the stage. The Queen and Prince Philip were due to catch a barge along the river to their next engagement. As they made their way towards it, we came into their line of sight and Her Majesty beckoned us towards them.

The Red Devils looked uncertainly at each other. This wasn't part of the script. Then we looked back at the Queen standing fifty metres away from us. And then, without waiting for a command and with all semblance of military order thrown out of the window, we started walking towards her. We all wanted to have a bit of face time with the Queen, so each of us was checking his mates out of the corner of his eye, trying to cover the distance a little bit quicker than the others, without looking as if we were trying to rush. It must have appeared to an onlooker like a rather disorganized walking race as we all tried to get to Her Majesty first and be the one that got to speak to her.

None of us, though, was singled out. We ended up in a neat military line, standing to attention, while the Queen asked us polite, inconsequential questions about where we came from. We replied with due deference, and before long the royal party was off, leaving a band of happy, adrenalin-fuelled Red Devils, high from an exciting jump and from meeting the most famous woman in the world. It was a proud moment for me, and not bad for a lad from Toton who once doubted whether he'd ever be able to parachute again.

On another occasion Richard Branson was throwing a garden party at his home in Oxfordshire for all his employees. It was an amazing Georgian house with fantastic gardens and a big lake, all set in the most beauti-ful, rolling countryside. Our landing area was on the far side of the lake from the house, on a hillside. We landed successfully and got down on one knee, as we normally did, ready to come to attention. Suddenly we saw someone emerge from the distance, soaking wet and bedraggled, and start running up towards us. It was Richard Branson, who'd been hurled into the water by his staff, and he was carrying one of his kids in his arms. I suppose we should have predicted that meeting this particular dignitary would have been somewhat unconventional: rather than wait for us to march to him in a regimented line, he just ran to each of us individually to chat: 'All right, lads … come on, let's get you a beer.' So we went and joined in the party. Normally the Red Devils in their smart red jump-suits are the most distinctive-looking members of any crowd. Not here. Businessmen in pinstriped three-piece suits stood alongside the most flamboyant punk-rockers I'd ever seen. We were even introduced to Kylie Minogue. And Branson had more aeronautical displays up his sleeve. He owned a hot-air balloon that was decorated to look like a cloud with a Virgin 747 flying through it. For this event he'd re-routed one of his actual 747s to fly behind the balloon, so it actually looked as though the plane was passing through it. Quite a display, and quite a party.

During the week, when you're neither doing displays nor practising, your time is well filled by the other side of being a Red Devil: raising funds. As it was in the early days, the team is still self-financing. The Army supplies the men on full pay, the accommodation, and the team rooms in Aldershot where we ran things and kept our kit. But we had to supply our own aircraft and equipment – including the parachutes. To keep an aircraft going is an expensive business. After a certain number of hours in the air, the engines of our Islanders had to be stripped down and rebuilt; and fuel is very expensive. Nowadays the team charters a plane for each jump, but back then we had to maintain our own aircraft. The team would charge a fee for any public display, but that didn't do much more than cover the costs of the jump. Most of the equipment, with the exception of the parachutes, we made ourselves. As a trained parachute rigger I was very involved in this, and the flipside of the excitement of skydiving was a lot of long hours hunched over a sewing machine, manufacturing all manner of kit. Most of our funds, though, were raised by holding parachuting courses. There seemed to be an inexhaustible supply of men and women wanting to come and skydive with the Red Devils – including people as diverse as Jim Davidson, Matthew Kelly, Colin Baker, Ian Ogilvy and Philip Schofield.

We'd run courses in the evenings and at weekends, during which time the students would receive training very similar to what I'd undergone at Brize Norton, before performing a static-line jump or, later in my time with the team, a tandem jump, when they would jump strapped to one of us. All the team were keen to become parachute jump instructors. I got as far as being what was known as a potential instructor – rather like a student instructor, who can teach only under supervision – and I'd have loved to carry on and become a fully fledged parachute instructor. The idea of teaching, of passing on the things I'd been fortunate enough to learn, appealed to me. But there were only so many hours in the day. With all the displays and the rigging, not to mention a young family at home, my legs simply couldn't manage it, so I let the teaching drop.

Once a year the team would take part in a BA Dreamflight, where a plane full of disabled children would be taken out to Orlando in Florida and have a holiday at Disneyworld, escorted by a few of the Red Devils. That was one of the few jobs, though, that I left to the other guys. I didn't want to put myself in a position where *I* was needing to be put into a wheelchair as well as the kids I was supposed to be looking after!

There was a lot of friendly rivalry between Army parachute teams – especially between the Marines and the Red Devils – about who could, for example, create the biggest stack, and so we were always trying to make our canopy relative work bigger and better. In addition to this, however, some members of the team – the crème de la crème – entered a lot of actual skydiving competitions, but the level of training was so intense that I was just not capable on my legs of putting in that kind of intense work, so I never really ventured into the realms of competitive jumping.

Occasionally, though, just for the hell of it, we would enter a competition. This would involve the judges giving each participating team a certain number of formations that we had to execute in the air as precisely as possible. They would be watching from the ground using binoculars. The ability of some of the guys was truly amazing. In the accuracy competitions the judges would place an electronic ten-centimetre-diameter disc on the ground, and some competitors had the ability to put their heel onto this nearly every jump. Some of the guys would cut down the heel of the shoes, or fix a chiselled-down rubber doorstop to their heels, so that they could land precisely on the centre of the disc time after time. Their skill was amazing.

My history of competition jumping had not been entirely without incident. Back in Cyprus the staff at the parachute centre had entered the Rhine Army Parachute Competition. This involved three days' training before it even started. On the last jump of the third day I suffered a rotating malfunction. I cut myself away and opened the reserve chute. These back-up canopies are designed to inflate very quickly – as you might be quite close to the ground when you open them, you need to have a good, positive opening. I certainly got that. As the chute inflated, my whole body jerked and my false leg shot off my stump, out of my trousers, and went spinning down to earth! I didn't know where to look: upwards, to check my chute had properly opened, or down, to watch where my leg was falling – into a forestry block near the drop zone.

There were a lot of people down on the DZ – spectators, judges, other teams from all over Europe. I managed to land on one leg in the pit, then waited while someone fetched me some crutches from the medical centre. Once I was mobile, an announcement came over the Tannoy: 'Ladies and gentlemen, could we please have some volunteers to search for Paul's leg, which came off in the last jump.'

Since it was a military event, the volunteers approached it with military organization. They formed an extended line and entered the forest like beaters at a grouse shoot. Happily this was when I had painted my leg bright red, so it stood out among the foliage and they found it. The leg was a bit smashed and split, but an aircraft engineer took it away and knocked it into good enough shape for me to wear it, even though the foot was held on with masking tape. It was too badly damaged to put much weight on it, and it made a hideous noise, but at least I was able to carry on with the jumping. There is a kind of system of fines in skydiving: my fine that day was two crates of beer for the reserve ride, and one for the first time a leg had come off in freefall. Everyone drank the beer while I repacked my main and reserve chutes.

This was an international competition, and the Germans had provided a Jolly Green Giant helicopter. A Sea King variant, this is one of the biggest and most impressive helicopters in the world, and the Cyprus team was allowed to use it for the rest of the competition because of my having trouble with my leg. It was a great aircraft to jump from, with a big tailgate, and because I performed the required number of jumps that week from a German military aircraft, I became eligible for my German wings, with which I was presented at the end of the competition. The first limbless Para to get foreign limbs. Worth losing a leg for!

Moments like that aside, I tended to steer clear of competitions, especially once I'd joined the Red Devils. Not only would the extra training put too much strain on my leg, but I felt it would take some of the enjoyment out of the sport. To reach that kind of level you have to be deadly serious about it, and really I just wanted my jumping to be fun. All things considered, I was more than pleased with what I'd achieved, and rather than bust a gut to get to the very highest level of the sport, I was happy just to enjoy it to the best of my ability. To be the best I could possibly be, rather than push myself to be better than everyone else. To accept my limitations.

Being in the Red Devils was such a happy period in my life. I loved my job and I loved being a dad – both of which I would never have guessed would be possible as I lay broken and wounded in hospital in Woolwich. My kids – Ben, who had been born in Cyprus; Georgina, who came into the world eleven months later; and John, who was born in 1989 – were a particular joy. Sheila adored being a mum and concentrated her time and energy on that. The nature of the Red Devils' work meant that I was busy for a lot of weekends, and especially bank holiday weekends, so we missed out on a lot of holiday time. But because of my family commitments, as well as the strain on my leg, I didn't do all the displays, and I treasured every moment I spent with the kids.

When they were very little I was there doing the nappies and night feeds; and when they were older I would sneak off with them to the park early in the morning at weekends, leaving Sheila to lie in. I loved clambering over the climbing frame with them, letting them pursue adventurous enterprises that their mum wouldn't have been able to watch for fear that they'd fall. And when the time came to teach them to swim, I'd get them to jump into the deep end with their arms straight, then push themselves up to the surface and clamber out, before taking it in turns to hang onto my shoulders while I did lengths. I wanted them to be filled with confidence, and it paid dividends. When Ben was 10 he took part in the swimathon at the local pool. I had to tell him to stop after 110 lengths, and I had to pull him out of the water still wanting to do more. And when the boys were older, I used to take them climbing at an indoor climbing centre. As an amputee I drew some strange looks, but I didn't want to let my injuries get in the way of the kids having fun, so I learned to scale the walls with the best of them.

I remember, when I was 7 or 8, there was a boy with a false leg who used to walk to a school near where I lived. This was in the 1960s, so his leg was even more archaic than my early ones. All the kids used to take the mickey out of him, following him down the street and calling him Peg-leg. Even those who didn't make fun of him couldn't help staring, because he just looked so different. When my kids were born I think part of me always worried that the same sort of stigma that poor boy suffered would some-how be transferred to Ben, Georgina and John.

I needn't have worried. The Warrenpoint bombings happened long before any of my children were born, so they all grew up seeing me and my problems as being normal. Because I did everything I could to make our lives as ordinary as possible – it wasn't as if I was in and out of institutions, or surrounded myself with other amputees

– they never really came across anybody with similar injuries; but because they were used to everything about me, this was never a problem. In fact I think it made them better kids – more aware and tolerant of anybody with a disability. All three of them have grown from being caring, understanding children into being caring, understanding adults. When they were young I don't think they were ever teased because their dad had a funny leg. On the contrary, I used to go to their junior school with my parachute and my Red Devil gear and give talks for the kids, and I hope that I managed to turn around what could have been a negative into a positive: I wasn't a disabled dad, I was a Red Devil with a robot leg who jumped out of airplanes.

Sometimes, of course, my injury couldn't help but get in the way of things we wanted to do. If we visited a museum or an amusement park, say, there were times when I would stubbornly refuse to use a wheelchair, even though my legs were in great pain from walking around, and it was affecting everyone else's enjoyment. Wheelchairs were anathema to me. I wasn't a paraplegic, so I didn't feel that I really deserved the use of one. Even more than that, I felt like sitting in a wheelchair was some sort of admission of failure. Gradually, though, I realized that my stubbornness was having a negative effect on my family and others around me. Everyone – including the children – could see that I was in pain. Through my own ignorance I was stopping them from enjoying themselves. It's amazing how often children can teach you something about yourself. Mine certainly did. As soon as they persuaded me to use a wheelchair, the stigma fell away. The kids could take turns sitting on my lap, and everyone was much happier.

When the children asked what had happened to my leg – which of course they all did at different points in time as they grew up and became more inquisitive – I tried to explain it all to them honestly, but in terms that they could easily understand: there had been a big explosion, and Daddy had been injured. They didn't need to know about politics, or about the guys who had died, or months in hospital and rehab. Why fill their heads with such things? Things blowing up they understood from TV, but the trauma that goes with it was too much for their young minds. And rather than dwell on the negative side of having lost my leg, I dwelt on the positive: I was lucky enough to have a new one, and be able to stay in the Army. I never wanted to appear disconsolate or grumpy about what had happened – partly because that's just the way I am, but also because I didn't want my past to affect my kids' outlook on life. Much better if I could make what happened to me a positive learning experience for them.

I spent six years all told with the Red Devils. During the first few years I did everything I could to match the other guys in the team jump for jump. As time went on, however, I found the pressure on my legs was starting to tell. The time spent in the air was fine. More than fine, because it was then that I was the equal of anyone else. And I was always very careful to walk away from jumps when the wind was too treacherous or there was rain or low cloud: I couldn't afford to have a heavy landing that would damage my leg. To hurt yourself doing something essential is one thing; to sustain damage when you're supposedly having fun would just be daft, so I approached my skydiving very responsibly.

However, the business of walking to the aircraft, walking back from the drop zone and packing my parachute started to take its toll. My leg was forever breaking down and I was in constant pain, practically living off anti-inflammatory tablets. I was pig-headed, refusing to make allowances for myself. If the team needed to carry heavy parachutes from the store to the van, I would have to do my bit so that nobody thought I was slacking. I didn't want to be seen as a token team member, unable and unwilling to pull my weight. I'd worked hard to get where I was, and I had no intention of not doing my bit.

My attitude made for some frustrating and painful moments, moments when I had to remind myself of the promise I'd made after Warrenpoint. I'd vowed that I would live my life to its fullest, to make up for the lives lost by my friends. What would they give to be doing what I was doing now, pain or no pain, frustration or no frustration? The memory of them, and I suppose the guilt of being a survivor, drove me on. I wasn't going to sit on my bum feeling sorry for myself and let the world go by.

But it couldn't last for ever. Towards the end we went on a team training week, during which time we were doing eight jumps a day. That's quite a physical task, but I managed to keep up with the guys with the exception of one jump when I hit my head rushing to enter the plane. In the evenings, though, when the lads disappeared down to the local bars, I had to go to bed, exhausted and in pain from the effort. It was then, I think, that I realized I couldn't keep going with the Red Devils indefinitely, because it was becoming ever more difficult for me to keep up with the able-bodied paratroopers.

It took a while for me to come to this realization, to admit to what I saw as my weaknesses. Even now, it's something I don't like to do – I'd rather end up sore and tired than bow out of something I want to do – but back then this feeling was more pronounced. I didn't want anybody to think that I was using my injuries as an excuse to skive off and avoid doing as much work as they were doing. Fortunately I could achieve a great deal with the team with my parachute rigging, which involved a lot of sitting down, and as time went by I found myself doing more of this and less of the running, jumping, and carrying heavy weights.

Gradually I moved from being a full-time jumper for the Red Devils to being a full-time rigger. I suppose there must have been a part of me that felt regretful about not jumping so much, but in the end I simply had to be practical. There was only so much that my legs would let me do, and on the positive side I'm sure my family preferred it now that I wasn't obliged to be away every weekend, and wasn't coming home a total wreck every night. As always, I tried to look on the positive side. I'd achieved something I'd set my heart on, and that felt good. But I'd also gained the self-confidence to say when something was too much for me, and learned a little about my limitations. I just hoped they wouldn't stop me from doing what I wanted to do in the future.

Chapter Nine

The Wrong Way Round

In May 1989, four years after joining the Red Devils, the Army sent me once again on loan to the Joint Services Adventure Training Centre in Cyprus, my second two-year posting there. I moved out with our little family, and our third child, John, was born a little while after we arrived. We would do lots of parachuting displays for different events – UN medal parades, annual military shows, and some displays on the beach, which has to be the best place to land – but the pace was less intense than it ever was with the Red Devils, and more manageable for me.

I was happy to be back in Cyprus. In the military parachuting world there aren't many sunshine destinations. Cyprus is one of the few, and it was good to return to the parachute school. My family enjoyed it too, I think. It was a great environment for them to grow up in, being able to go to the beach every afternoon. At the parachute school we'd have the wheels off the ground at seven o'clock every morning because, Cyprus being an island, the winds started to get up around midday, making parachuting hazardous. For this reason we tended to knock off early in the afternoon, so I was able to join the family and spend precious, happy time with the children. Nowadays the resort of Ayia Napa is party central. When I was there it was just a sleepy village with a fantastic beach, and in many ways we felt like we were on a permanent holiday. A constant stream of family and friends came out to stay.

All holidays come to an end, however. My two-year deployment in Cyprus passed quickly. When we returned to the UK I found myself back in the rigging room for the Red Devils. I'd hardly been back, however, before John Ricks, the former Red Devil who had introduced me to the square parachute that had allowed me to do my first land jump, made me an offer I couldn't refuse.

I hadn't been intending to leave the Army just yet. The Parachute Regiment had been good to me, and although my injuries meant I was unable to do the kind of soldiering I had wanted to do ever since I played with my Action Man as a small boy, I felt very grateful that the military had kept me on, given me a role and the chance to gain qualifications, and allowed me to feel useful. But I knew that I would have to leave the Army at some stage. Moreover, it was no secret that many ex-servicemen find themselves back in civvy street not knowing what to do with themselves. It was always a worry that the transition to civilian life would be even worse for me, given my injuries, and I'd always rather assumed that the opportunities for an amputee in the commercial world would be somewhat limited.

But when John, who was in charge of research and development for GQ Parachutes – a company that dated back to the barnstorming age of civil aviation – offered me a job on the strength of my experience in rigging and sport parachuting, I suddenly realized that there might be other opportunities available to me. Other paths I could take. And although leaving the Army was a hard decision to make in some respects – I had, after all, been involved with it ever since I was a cadet at the age of 11 – I was keen to take the next step up in my skydiving career. I accepted John's offer.

I was discharged from the British Army on 6 October 1991 with a grading of 'exemplary conduct'. I felt I was able to look back over my time in the Parachute Regiment with pride. It was true that I had suffered a terrible injury, but I was unable to feel bitter or negative about it. In life you have to play the cards you're dealt, and I hope my commanding officer's testimony in my Certificate of Service reflects that I tried to play the best hand I could:

LCpl Burns has completed 13 years' service with the Parachute Regiment. He has completed duty tours in Berlin, West Germany, Cyprus and Northern Ireland. LCpl Burns is very experienced in the world of freefall parachuting, being a very competent parachutist himself and an advanced rigger. In addition he has many broader based skills and was able to manage a workshop handling both stores and facilities, without supervision, to the highest standard. He can train and instruct extremely well and has a good, relaxed manner enabling him to relate easily to senior and subordinate personnel alike. His conduct throughout his career has been exemplary.

The nature of my new job meant that I wasn't entirely divorced from the Army. At one point during my time at GQ Parachutes there were five former Red Devils working for the company, and working in the parachuting world meant you always had links of some sort with the military. Over the following years I would do most of my recreational jumping from a military parachute centre. Their years in the Army are an important time in the life of any ex-serviceman or woman, and I think that to have had no more connection with the military would have been a terrible wrench for me.

My work at GQ Parachutes – as a project engineer and workshop manager for the whole research and development department – was varied. At the time they held the contract to supply all the UK's special forces with parachutes, just like the one that had allowed me to start jumping. These parachutes would be slightly different, depending on their usage: HALO (high-altitude, low-opening), HAHO (high-altitude, high-opening), and LALO (low-altitude, low-opening) chutes all had their various quirks, and our job was to try to continually improve them. We also worked on improving the company's line of round parachutes. These still tended to be used by most of the military because they are so much simpler – you don't need to teach the troops the intricacies of flying a square parachute. We also worked on a line of ejector-seat canopies, as there's no point ejecting a pilot from an aircraft if he can't get safely back down to earth. We constructed air-sea rescue harnesses, as well as slightly weirder and more wonderful projects like a remote-controlled parachute system, and a special camouflaged parachute for the agents of America's Drug Enforcement Administration to use in undercover stings.

Working for GQ was a sea change for me. While I'd been in the Army, skydiving had been part of my job, and there was plenty of time to do it. Now I was in a factory and office, and while there was a little bit of jumping to be done as part of my new position, I wasn't really fit enough to carry out the hard-core test jumping that goes hand in hand with devising and improving parachute designs. So I just kept the skydiving ticking along – a few jumps here and there, sometimes with a little civilian display team called the Skydiving Spectaculars run by John Dod, but just enough, really, to stay current. It didn't feel so bad to back off from it a little. I had, after all, done a *lot* of skydiving over the past few years.

My life was filled with work and family commitments. I bought an old Harley-Davidson, which gave me a bit of a buzz on the commute to work each day – the motorbike licence I'd got out in Cyprus meant I no longer had to stay offroad as I had done with the trike down in Netheravon.

I loved that Harley, not because it was big and shiny, but because it was very comfortable for me to sit on given my injuries. I decided to keep it secret from my mum, knowing how worried the idea of me on a motorbike would make her. She'd been distraught about the idea even when I was able-bodied. I was rumbled, though, when I was talking to my nephew in front of her one day. 'How's the Harley, Uncle Paul?' he asked. Mum couldn't believe her ears, and from that point on she would worry not only about the things I had told her about, but also the things I hadn't told her about. I don't blame her for those anxieties. She's lived with her son being injured for so long, and as a parent I can understand how much my being blown up must have occupied her mind. The reality was, though, that with three young children I didn't really have the time to go thrill-seeking, but I think that in Mum's head I was pulling wheelies along the motorway every day of the week!

There were down sides to my new position at GQ Para-chutes. My last job had been in Cyprus, where I had been in a position to manage my own time and workload around my injuries. I knew how long I could be on my feet before the pain in my legs became unbearable, and I could arrange my workload accordingly. Working at GQ was different. All of a sudden I had to be at work before everybody else, and leave after them. I was on my feet a lot more than I wanted to be – my office was upstairs and the workshop downstairs – and this took its toll on my body. I found myself having to take more and more painkillers, just to manage the pain. When I came home I had to do all the little jobs that most people perform without thinking – cutting the grass, going to the supermarket, taking the kids out and about. Before, I'd been able to manage these jobs, but now, with the effect work was having on my body, they became increasingly difficult.

After about two years at GQ, I entered a downhill spiral. I would take painkillers before getting up in the morning, just to mask the pain from the damage I'd done the previous day. It's very hard getting out of bed in the morning knowing that as soon as you put weight on your feet it will hurt you. I was constantly blocking the pain with drugs, and the worse the pain grew, the stronger the drugs had to be. With no flesh and grafted skin on my stump and a consistently broken heel, that pain could be considerable just from the pressure of standing, let alone walking. I seemed to be continually in and out of the limb centre, getting new legs with constant modifications, but although the technology of prosthetic limbs was getting better all the time, these limbs remained fairly basic and not one of them was able to stop the incessant pain I was feeling. It was then, as it is now, very hard to make a prosthetic limb that fits me well and allows me to do normal, everyday things

without pain and without skin breaking down somewhere on my stump.

I kept quiet about my discomfort. I didn't want people
to think I was making a fuss, or trying to get out of
working, or using my disability as some kind of excuse.
Every day I would get into the car, or onto my bike, and
drive to the factory in Woking; every day I would spend
more time on my feet than was good for me; and every
day the pain got a little bit worse. I tried to stay cheerful
and to pretend that everything was all right, but there
were moments of great frustration. When I look back on
that time I don't remember being aware of not putting a
brave face on things, but sometimes you don't always see
yourself the way other people see you. Being in that
much pain is bad for your body, but it doesn't do your
brain much good either. I'm sure, looking back, that there
must have been times when I was difficult to be around,
even though I was doing my best to be laid-back about
things and not let my physical condition become too
much of an issue.

When I went to my local GP, it wasn't because I
thought he'd be able to make me better. My body was
broken; everything that *could* be fixed *had* been. All I
wanted was some more powerful painkillers, something to
mask the pain so that I could just keep going with my life.

The GP took one look at me. 'I'm going to sign you off,'
he said.

I raised an eyebrow and wondered how long he was
talking about. A week or two, maybe – long enough to

have a bit of a rest, catch up with things at home that seemed to be mounting up, and for the pain in my legs to subside a little. That would have been fantastic. I'd be able to go back to work refreshed, and I started to relax a little at the thought. The doctor filled in a form and handed it to me. 'Come and see me in six months' time.'

I blinked as I realized what he was saying. My GP wasn't signing me off for two weeks or even a couple of months. He was signing me off permanently. 'There are people far better off healthwise than you who aren't working,' he told me. 'You simply don't *have* to work. You've done your bit.'

I guess the doctor was doing his best to convince me that it was OK not to be working. I still felt like someone had hit me over the head with a hammer. I'd *always* worked. As a kid I'd done paper rounds and earned extra money washing cars. From the moment I left school I'd had a job in the Army. Even after I was blown up, my single focus had been to get back to work, not to let my injuries stop me from doing my bit.

Now I was being told not only that I shouldn't work, but that I *couldn't* work.

It's no exaggeration to say that, after the dreadful events at Warrenpoint so many years before, this was the second biggest blow of my life. I was of a class of person that *had* to be busy, to feel that I was pulling my weight and doing something constructive with my life. I was mentally driven to keep working; to be told I couldn't was a shock to the system.

There's a stigma attached to not working, and I found it difficult to stomach. I had made such a point of trying to live my life as an able-bodied person rather than a disabled one that being told I couldn't work because of my disability rather pulled the carpet from underneath me. Since the horror of Warrenpoint I'd turned my life around, made myself a valuable person and conquered my problems. I could be as good as anyone else at what I tried to do. I could bring in a wage. Only now, it seemed, I couldn't. I'd been pushing myself too much, both physically and mentally.

It would take a long time for me to get used to the idea. Even now, when people ask me what I do, I find it hard to answer that I'm medically retired. When I look at it objectively, though, I realize there was a tremendous amount of relief that I now no longer had to be running around all the time. It wasn't as if I didn't have lots to do with the family. And now it meant I could arrange my time around my legs, rather than have to live on painkillers. It was what I needed physically, and once I'd come to understand that, I was able to feel more positively about the path my life had taken.

It was a strange time when I left work. All of a sudden there was no pressure on me. And once I'd got past the stigma of being medically retired, I came to see how liberating it was to have the decision about whether to work or not to work taken away from me. It was such a privilege to be able to spend more time with the kids, to take them to school and pick them up again, and also to be able to pursue my other interests to whatever level I wanted. Sheila and I had more time to spend together, and I had more chance to see my wider family too. Now that I was a bit older, I understood that perhaps I should have given myself a bit more time to recuperate after getting out of rehab, rather than being so single-minded about going back to work in the first place. In a way I was owed a slightly easier time of it, and once I'd accepted that, things became easier.

I'm more comfortable now with the idea that I don't have to be defined by my job; comfortable with the idea that just being medically retired doesn't mean you do nothing. I am, for example, still an advanced parachute rigger. I keep my ratings up, and there are only a handful of us in the country. I'm a ski-bike instructor and a yacht-master cruising instructor. I'm lots of things, and probably have more skills than many able-bodied people.

And what was more, being medically retired was what allowed me to embark upon my next big adventure.

When I was in hospital in Woolwich, visitors came and went. Many of them were there to offer practical support; others just came along to keep me company. Often I'd never see them again.

One day a very nice, rather military chap came to visit me. He had a regimental badge on his blazer, grey hair, and to a kid like me he looked almost 100 years old. 'Don't worry,' he said in his rather patrician tones. 'We'll look after you. We'll see you're all right.'

He explained he was from a charity called Blesma, which meant nothing to me at the time. I thanked him politely, he went off, and – true to form – I never saw him again. It wasn't for some time that I fully understood the purpose of the charity which that nice old gentleman represented, and with which I am now involved.

Blesma is the British Limbless Ex Service Men's Association and they've been around since just after the First World War. We have a welfare network that looks after anybody who has lost a limb, whether while in service or subsequently through accident or illness or for whatever reason, and their wives and widows. In recent years the membership has been shrinking as the many amputees from the First and Second World Wars have died, and so we have been able to extend our reach to include those ex-servicemen and women who have not lost a limb but lost the use of one. All in all there are about 5,000 members. Blesma provides proactive, hands-on care for every member and their wives and widows, in contrast to charities such as the British Legion, which will provide assistance but don't necessarily know who needs it, and can only be of help if people go to them. As one of a number of Blesma's voluntary area welfare representatives, I look after the Guildford area, which means I'm in contact with all the local members, offering them practical support and help – from going up a ladder, if they need it, to advising them on their pension entitlements. Blesma exists solely for the welfare of its members, so we can be sure that there isn't a little old guy who lost an arm in Aden, destitute and unable to cope with his disability.

Blesma also offers active help with rehabilitation, and it was through this side of their activities that I first became involved with the charity. When they first visited me in hospital, I had the sense that it was, like the British Legion, very much a charity meant for veterans of the two World Wars. And with its name indicating that it was intended just for *ex*-servicemen, I didn't feel very comfortable about approaching them for help in any way. In those pre-Afghanistan days there were only a handful of amputees still serving in the Army, and I had the feeling that Blesma wasn't for us. I received the quarterly magazine regularly, though, and the occasional letter checking that I was all right. In return, I did a bit of fundraising for the association. When I was in Cyprus, for example, I did the annual Dhekelia mile-long sponsored swim on their behalf. A year later I got my diving qualification and did the whole thing again, but underwater this time – a big mistake, because it was one of the slowest, most painful things I've ever done, kicking away with one not so normal foot. When I eventually emerged from the Mediterranean, everyone had gone home apart from my family and friends. But as I was just getting on with my life – skydiving, raising a family, and doing all the things that I did – I really had very little to do with Blesma.

Then, in the mid-eighties, while I was jumping with the Red Devils, I was flicking through the Blesma newsletter when I noticed a list of events they were holding.

Blesma prides itself on providing events for its members who are not necessarily of the sedentary kind, and one of these events was sailing at Cowes Week. I immediately thought that I'd like to do that – my life had been so full of parachuting that it would be good to try something new – so I put my name down. I was given a place, the Red Devils gave me the time off work, and soon enough I found myself in the sleepy little town of Cowes, which, once a year, transforms itself to host the biggest sailing regatta of its kind in the world.

As there are over 1,000 races, the town becomes jam-packed with boats and yachtsmen, and the sea is like Piccadilly Circus. At least, it rather seemed like that to me at the time because I didn't know one end of a boat from the other. I'd never been sailing before, had no idea what was involved, and all of a sudden I found myself on a 32-foot Westerly yacht with seven or eight Blesma guys who all seemed a great deal older than me. Some had served in the Second World War, some in Aden, but all of them had leg amputations, and none of them had any sailing qualifications. We had an able-bodied skipper on loan to us, but even so it was a steep learning curve as we took to the crowded waters of the Solent.

I was very taken with the sport of sailing. For one thing, it was sociable – the races were organized to start at a decent hour and finish in time for Pimm's o'clock – but it was also very exciting. When you have twenty large yachts all screaming to be the first round a buoy out in the open sea, it can be very nerve-racking. It was exactly my kind of thing, although I was amazed by the resilience of some of the older guys on the boat, whose capacity for a hard day's sailing was matched only by their capacity for a hard evening's drinking. I recall a number of hungover mornings that week.

Cowes Week was a brilliant experience that I really enjoyed, but my life revolved around skydiving and I didn't sail again until I was working at GQ Parachutes. Really it was only ever a distraction, fun to do now and then. I got my competent crew and radio qualifications, but sailing was never really a big part of my life.

I did, however, make a few friends through my Blesma sailing. One of the volunteer skippers who used to take us out was a fantastic guy called Colin Lloyd. Colin was a former superintendent of the Metropolitan Police and had served with SO19, the Met's armed response unit. While chasing a villain he'd jumped off a wall, and in doing so snapped both his Achilles tendons, which meant he'd been retired early. Colin's passion was sailing and, now that he had more free time, he was able to indulge that passion, and he used to help out the Blesma sailors by skippering their boats. He later died of cancer – a tragic loss of a lovely man. Nigel Smith had joined the Royal Navy at 16. Like me, he had always wanted a career in the armed forces; like mine, that career was prematurely ended when, 18 and stationed in Cyprus, he was hit by a drunk driver. Nigel was severely injured in the accident, and had to have his right leg amputated above the knee. Dave Baker was a tank operator with a similar story: he had been knocked off his motorbike – it's amazing how many people lose limbs this way.

Colin, Dave, Nigel and I got into the habit of going together round the annual London Boat Show at Earls Court, just to wander about looking at the boats and meet up with people we knew from the sailing world. Nothing ever came of these shows, really – they were more an excuse for a day out than anything else – but when the 1996 Boat Show came around in the January of that year, things turned out to be a little bit different.

The four of us met up at the show, as we normally did. Outside Earls Court, we saw a boat too big to fit into the exhibition halls. It was the most beautiful vessel, and we were awestruck. It was there to advertise a race called the BT Global Challenge – a round-the-world yacht race run by a former Parachute Regiment officer by the name of Sir Chay Blyth. Obviously that piqued my interest. Blyth was quite a figure. In the 1960s he had rowed with one other man across the Atlantic Ocean; and in the 1970s he had become the first person to sail round the world westward, and later skippered a crew of paratroopers to success in another round-the-world race.

Round-the-world races are generally reserved for people at the top of the sailing tree. To go on one of these expeditions requires years of experience and a high level of skill. But the race Chay Blyth was promoting wasn't for professionals – it was for ordinary people with limited sailing experience. Blyth had successfully masterminded a similar race four years previously – the British Steel

Challenge – and now he was promoting another of these great adventures. And the lack of professional crews wasn't the only unique thing about the BT Global Challenge.

In the late 1960s Chay Blyth had a dream to become the first person to sail single-handed round the globe, but he was pipped to the post by Robin Knox-Johnston. Undeterred, Blyth decided that he would try to enter the record books by doing the same thing – only he would circumnavigate the globe in the opposite direction. To sail westward round the earth is a very different undertaking. Knox-Johnston's route took advantage of the prevailing winds and currents, just as all the sailors of old had done. Blyth's route, on the other hand, took him *against* the prevailing wind. To a yachtsman, this is sailing the 'wrong way' round the world, and the BT Global Challenge, unlike the other big races such as the Whitbread Round the World Race, was also to go the wrong way round.

But really this was only of passing interest to me. Such events were only for able-bodied crew. I left Chay Blyth to promote his expedition, and wandered with my friends into the busy hubbub of the exhibition centre. We strolled around, idly browsing the different stands and exhibits and looking admiringly at the shiny boats, knowing that they were all entirely out of our reach but enjoying window-shopping anyway. After a while we found ourselves at the Guinness stand, which is often a very crowded meeting point. It was near here that I noticed a stand promoting Chay Blyth's Global Challenge race, and I saw that they were still trying to recruit for a boat that had been entered for the event and was called *Time and Tide*. This yacht wasn't like the others in the race: it was to be manned by an all-disabled crew, or a crew made up of those who had suffered life-threatening illnesses like cancer.

There are not a huge amount of people who want to go sailing round the world. Of those who *do* want to go sailing round the world, there are not a lot who can. And of those who *can*, not a lot of them are disabled. And of those who are disabled, there aren't a lot who can take ten months out of their life to do it. It was not surprising, then, that the race organizers were struggling to find a crew for *Time and Tide*. They were short of four members and it was less than nine months to go until the off – this being January and the race starting in September. So, when the organizers manning the stand saw Colin, Dave, Nigel and me limping towards them, they must have thought all their Christmases had come at once.

Like fishermen trying to hook a fish, they started giving us the spiel about what an amazing race it was, what a life-enhancing and life-changing experience. The whole point about the Global Challenge was that you didn't have to have any experience, just an interest in sailing. But the fact that we'd *had* a little bit of experience made us ideal. The people manning that stand didn't even have to give it a moment's thought – they wanted us on that boat.

Some decisions in life come about as a result of long and careful consideration. Others are made on the hoof, in the heat of the moment. This was one of those decisions. 'If it's OK with my wife Sheila,' I heard myself saying, 'then I'll do it.'

The instant I said that, they started reeling me in. I had to meet Chay Blyth, they told me, and arranged a meeting for two o'clock that afternoon. Colin, Dave, Nigel and I had a quick liquid lunch, during which we mulled over the prospect of joining the race. Clearly it was a big thing to take on: ten months away from home, and all the build-up beforehand. It also involved raising a race fee of £18,750. Colin and Dave quickly decided that it wasn't for them, but Nigel and I were still keen, and a couple of hours later we found ourselves on the yacht outside Earls Court, being interviewed by this legend of the Parachute Regiment.

Sir Chay Blyth was a no-nonsense, businesslike character. He had to be. The presence of *Time and Tide* on the Global Challenge – a boat full of inexperienced, disabled sailors – was a big risk for him, and a big anxiety. The Global Challenge was being billed as the toughest yacht race yet devised. If anything went wrong – and it was entirely possible that something *would* go wrong – Chay would have to carry the can. He was very astute, and as he questioned us about our suitability for the race, I had the impression that not much got past him. At the end of that interview, somewhat to our amazement, we were accepted onto the crew. Moreover, as our limited sailing history would make us some of the most experienced crew members on the boat, we were destined to be watch leaders, each able to take charge of one of the shifts that would keep it sailing twenty-four hours a day.

On the train journey back home I felt slightly dazed, not quite sure what it was that I'd let myself in for. More importantly, I wasn't quite sure how I was going to break the news of my eventful day's work to my wife!

I had made it clear to Chay and everyone else involved in the race that I would only join up if Sheila gave me her blessing. With three kids at home, I was quite well aware of the sacrifices I was asking my family to make. I would be making them too: children grow up quickly, and to miss out on a chunk of their childhood like that was not, I knew, a casual undertaking. This couldn't be my decision. It had to be *our* decision. When I got home I sat down with Sheila and explained what had happened. 'It's a once in a lifetime opportunity,' I told her, and it was true: the chances of there being another disabled circumnavigation of the globe were minuscule. And even if the chance did come round again, I knew that as time progressed, the chances of my being able to take part would only grow smaller as my body succumbed more and more to my injuries. It was more important for me than for most other people to grab whatever opportunities came my way. 'So what do you think?' I said. 'Will you support me? Can I go?'

Sheila could have said no, and if she had I genuinely would have put the whole idea out of my mind. But I think she saw how much it meant to me, and I think she saw that, far from abandoning the children, what I really wanted to do was make this as positive an experience for them as possible: I'd be able to come home for a bit when the ship was in port; we got a new computer, so they'd be able to track my progress; I would write a diary to send home to them regularly; and most importantly, it could be an inspirational achievement for them as well as me. I could make sure everything was properly in place so that this wasn't just my adventure, it was the whole family's.

Sheila said yes. Perhaps she felt she had to. Perhaps, when she realized how much this would mean to me, she had no choice. Perhaps it wasn't fair of me to place that difficult decision at her door. But although as the race grew nearer she became increasingly eager for me to change my mind about the whole thing – she feared for my health and worried how she and the children would cope without me for so long – from the moment she green-lit the expedition she was never anything other than entirely supportive. In fact she was more than that: Sheila would be instrumental in the long months of fund-raising that were to follow, and of course while I was away the running of the family would be her responsibility. I'll always be grateful to her for that.

As for me, in the days after that visit to the Boat Show, I knew that I had only a short amount of time to prepare for my biggest challenge yet.

Chapter Ten

Preparing for the Race

Since becoming medically retired I was living off my war and Army pensions, and the compensation money I'd received after my accident had been invested in a house. It meant we had enough to get by on, but it was hardly a fortune and there was never a great deal of money sloshing around. Certainly not enough for me to be able to find in my back pocket the £18,750 each crew member had to raise to buy their berth on *Time and Tide*.

Fundraising for the race had been a constant problem for the organizers. The brain behind the idea of raising an all-disabled crew to sail round the world was the man who was to skipper the boat, James Hatfield. James had been born with a hole in the heart. In 1975, aged 19, he had been out jogging when he ruptured his aorta. Two years later he was in hospital having undergone a fearsome number of open-heart surgery operations, which had left him with a body criss-crossed by a network of scars.

While he was convalescing, his brother brought him a big pile of magazines to help him pass the time. One of these magazines was *Yachting Monthly*.

James had never sailed before. But as he lay in his hospital bed flicking through this magazine, he came across an article about single-handed transatlantic yacht races. It caught his imagination and he decided there and then that he would enter one of these races. He was as good as his word, starting work on the project the moment he left hospital. Realizing that he couldn't afford to buy a boat, he made one himself and, just a few months after leaving hospital, had his first crack at sailing the Atlantic. Forty-eight hours into the race, he had already capsized twice, hit a whale, broken his hand, and encountered screaming 60 mph winds. James returned to England to find out that two of the contestants in the race had died during those storms.

He wasn't put off. A series of dangerous sailing expeditions followed, culminating in his sailing single-handed round the world, raising £360,000 for heart disease research in the process. In 1987 he had been voted Yachtsman of the Year and awarded an MBE for services to sailing and charity. Now he wanted to circumnavigate the globe with an all-disabled crew. He soon found out that having the idea is one thing; making it happen is quite another.

It's expensive to take a crew round the world: the boat has to be chartered, the price of stopover accommodation has to be met, and there are lots of other expenses, which meant that £600,000 was needed to get the boat into the water. The able-bodied crews found fundraising easier, I suppose because there was less of a stigma attached to them, or because the likelihood of something going wrong with their boats was smaller. When I first learned of the race in January 1996, there was still a great deal of money left to raise, so it was clear how important it was for me to do my bit.

I knew I wouldn't get very far by following the traditional money-raising routes of sponsored swims and the like, so I had to think outside the box. I started writing letters to anybody and everybody I could think of that I'd come into contact with, especially during my time in the Red Devils. I knew that the wealthy people I was targeting would have a massive number of appeals crossing their desks, so I had to think of ways to make mine stand out.

I wrote to Margaret Thatcher. After the Warrenpoint bombing she'd come to visit me and the other survivors, but I'd been unconscious at the time. I reminded her of this, and asked whether she might consider a donation to my cause as a consolation for not having met her. A few weeks later I received a cheque from her charitable foundation for £1,000.

I wrote a similar letter to Richard Branson, reminding him of the time I'd jumped into his back garden with the Red Devils. I had a suspicion that he might be sympathetic to my cause because Chay Blyth had been involved in his two attempts to break the world record speed for sailing the Atlantic, the second of which was successful. Sure enough, he was happy to make a donation.

Having had some success with one former Prime Minister, I had a go at raising some interest from another. Ted Heath was a famously keen yachtsman. In 1969 he had won the Sydney to Hobart Yacht Race; and while he was still Prime Minister he captained the winning British boat in the Admiral's Cup. In 1979 he took part in the Fastnet Race, which takes hundreds of yachts from Cowes to the tip of Ireland and back to Plymouth. The 1979 race was notorious. There were terrible storms, as a result of which the emergency services had to launch what was then the largest peacetime rescue operation. Fifteen people died, including one of the members of Ted Heath's boat. For me, being reminded of that race was a timely warning that sailing could be a hazardous sport and was not something to undertake lightly. And as the former PM would be only too aware of the dangers a disabled crew would face when sailing round the world, maybe he would consider sponsoring me.

I wrote to him, and received an invitation to tea. Heath lived in a lovely old house by Salisbury Cathedral called Arundells. The man I met, though, was not the vigorous sailor of old. He was getting on by this time, and even nodded off at one point during our meeting. Unfortunately he didn't feel able to sponsor me, but he gave me plenty of good advice and I got to meet one of the more colourful politicians of recent history.

Then I went through the *Sunday Times* Rich List and approached anybody with an interest in sailing. My biggest donors were Stannah Stairlifts in Andover, to whom I wrote not because I had need of their products but because the owners of the company, Brian and Alan Stannah, were sailing enthusiasts. Brian and Alan donated £3,000 each, and their staff raised an additional £3,000. This amounted to nearly half my berth fee. I was stunned by their generosity, and worried that they wouldn't get much in return for it. This didn't seem to concern them much. They were happy to use the trip as an incentive for their workforce, who would closely follow the race throughout its duration, and I also met their team when I finally reached Boston. As a way of saying thank you, their staff were allowed to have the use of *Time and Tide* for some sailing expeditions of their own.

I lost count of the number of letters I sent. As time went by, I accumulated a big file of rejections and a much, much smaller file of positive responses. The positives came from sources as diverse as the 10th Battalion of the Parachute Regiment and the Honourable Company of Fishmongers. Despite the generosity of my big donors, however, I was still some way off reaching my target. I had to think of another scheme to raise the cash that would enable me to take part in the race. Moreover, I felt bad about asking people for money without offering something in return. I felt there should be more in it for them, other than a dent in their bank balance. So I hit upon the idea of a raffle. What if I *could* offer something in return, something of value that my sponsors could have the chance of winning? As it happened, that something of value was sitting outside in the driveway.

I still had my Harley-Davidson. It was my pride and joy, really, but I'd have no need for it while I was ploughing through the Southern Ocean. So I decided to raffle it off. I made fifty tickets, costing £100 each, and offered these to smaller companies. A one-in-fifty chance, I told them, of winning a Harley. The uptake was good: I sold all the tickets and that was another £5,000 in the bank.

Some people, rather than offering me money, gave me donations in kind. Casio gave me a watch; Canon gave me a waterproof camera; BLOC eyewear donated sunglasses to me and the rest of the crew. A particular worry was medical equipment for the voyage. The first-aid supplies on *Time and Tide* would be for everybody's use, but I knew from experience that my 'good' leg would require constant attention. Even at the best of times, the grafted skin on my leg was prone to sores and infections. On the high seas, miles from any kind of proper medical care and in the harsh environments we could expect to encounter, these problems were going to be worse, not better. So I was glad when one company agreed to provide me with a year's worth of Mepore dressings – not something with which an able-bodied sailor would be particularly thrilled, but invaluable for me.

Over a period of a few months I managed to raise the £18,750 that I needed. While I and the rest of the crew were raising our berth fees, the charity that was putting *Time and Tide* in the water was busy raising the £600,000 required. It was a struggle. Whereas some of the other boats in the race had managed to find individual sponsors who covered the whole of this fee, the *Time and Tide* charity was obliged to piece together the funding from a number of different sources. Even when the race started it still hadn't quite raised all the money, so while the boat was going round the world, the charity continued wheeling and dealing so that we would have enough money to eat, and a bed to sleep in when we hit land. It was a stark contrast to some of the able-bodied boats, some of whose crews were reported to have been entertained in luxury hotels and fancy restaurants in the weeks preceding the race. I don't think that put any of our noses out of joint, though. It just made us more determined to see through what we'd started. And determination was a defining feature of the crew. We'd all had to struggle to make our way in the world. We'd all had obstacles to overcome. In many ways this made us more single-minded and desperate to succeed than an able-bodied crew.

I had things to think about other than money in the time leading up to the race. I was going to be away for the best part of a year, so I wanted to be sure that everything was properly set up at home. I wrapped presents and wrote cards for the kids' birthdays, knowing that I wouldn't be able to see them as they celebrated. I called the local florist to arrange that Sheila would have a bunch of flowers once a week. And because I knew that the expedition upon which I was about to embark was not without its risks, I made sure that my will was fully up to date and that Sheila had full access to all our bank accounts. Additionally, there was a certain amount of

press and publicity to be done for the race. As an amputee
I was one of the crew members whose disability was more
visible, and so there were a lot of photo shoots and journalists to deal with in order to raise publicity and awareness of race. We wanted to put across the point that it
wasn't a question of how disabled you are, but of how *able*
you are, and in so doing to put a lot of positivity back into
people's lives. The more evident disabilities got that point
over most efficiently. For that reason alone I was happy to
stick a pair of shorts on and have my false leg on display.

There was training too. *Time and Tide* was a 67-foot
boat, much bigger than anything I had ever sailed on
before and a quite different prospect from your average
32-foot cruising boat. With a bigger vessel the forces
involved are commensurately larger, and so is the potential danger. It was important that before we started we
had a working knowledge of our boat.

The Global Challenge organizers arranged a number
of sailing weekends where we could practise our skills
and meet up with members of the other boats. Because
the nature of the race was such that you didn't have to be
an experienced sailor to take part, all manner of person
congregated for that sail: doctors, nurses, firemen, milk-
men, farmers – you name it, they were there. People from
all walks of life and of all different ages, with different
levels of experience both in training and in life. The
organizers had divided all these people up into teams that
were as well balanced as possible. Each boat, for example,
needed somebody with a degree of medical experience,

whether that be a brain surgeon or a vet. The idea was to spread around the talents and make the playing field as level as possible.

Time and Tide was different, though. We couldn't cherry-pick the talents of a large pool of people because the criterion for joining the crew was to have been born with, or suffered in later life, some kind of disability. This meant that the range of our experiences was always pretty limited – yet another obstacle we would have to deal with as we made our way around the world. It was good, though, to meet some of our fellow competitors during training, and to get to know them as we learned the ins and outs of handling boats such as *Time and Tide*.

I realized that just changing sails on the boat, or putting in reefs – a way of reducing the size of a sail in order to slow it down in very high winds – involved enormous weights and forces. These would be difficult even for an able-bodied crew to handle; for us, doubly so. The boat's mast was eighty-four feet high, and there had to be crew members prepared to climb it. Not many people are blessed with a head for heights like that, especially in rolling seas; but with my skydiving experience I was happy enough to scale the mast with a climbing harness in order to check and repair the rig.

There were other, less nautical, aspects of being on a boat to get used to. Cooking for fourteen people on the tiny stove was almost as challenging as sailing the boat itself. There would be no room for any kind of refrigeration, so all our food would be freeze-dried. We'd have to get used to soaking dried meat overnight, and rehydrating dried vegetables in water. It was hardly the basis for weeks of gourmet cook-ups; on the positive side, the drab food would at least make us want to get to our destination quicker!

The training sails – one of which was along the 800-mile course of the Fastnet Race, in which Ted Heath had lost one of his crew in 1979 – brought home to me not only how challenging the race was going to be, but also the extent to which our disabilities would hinder us. It had been decided, for reasons of safety, that certain crew members would not be allowed to sail certain legs of the race. One person was told that they couldn't sail at all – a cruel blow at such a late stage. There was a starting crew of fourteen people, however, who – with the exception of one – intended to complete the whole course.

The skipper, James Hatfield, was one of these, of course; as were myself and my friend Nigel Smith, who had signed up at the same time as me. Chris Ogg was the First Mate. He was an experienced sailor and a senior manager for a delivery service, so he brought to the party both a wealth of sailing know-how and a precise, logistical mind. Six years previously Chris had received a diagnosis of Charcot-Marie-Tooth disease. This is a rare neurological disorder which, over time, can lead to wasting of the arms and legs. Chris had also lost the use of his right diaphragm, which meant he was highly prone to bronchial pneumonia; for him flu and even just the common cold were life-threatening illnesses. It took some

months for Chris to persuade his doctors to declare him
fit for all six legs of the voyage, and he needed to have a
constant supply of antibiotics, especially during the legs
that would take place in the inclement weather conditions
of the Southern Ocean.

Stuart Boreham was the first crew member to be
recruited onto *Time and Tide*, and he was one of the
representatives Nigel and I had met at the Boat Show.
Stuart was born with cerebral palsy, a motor condition
that limited his movement. Stuart had always been an
adventurous type, and had taken up motor racing as a
sport. He was no stranger to quirky endeavours, having
recently completed a charity race from John O'Groats to
Land's End – driving a ride-on lawnmower! And his
strength and willpower are such that subsequent to the
BT Global Challenge he rowed across the Atlantic, from
the Canary Islands to Barbados, single-handed. Four years
before the race, however, he had been involved in a go-kart
racing accident and damaged his leg. The surgeons had
inserted a metal plate and told him that if he ever broke
his leg again he would most likely lose it. And, as we were
to find out during the course of the race, such an injury
was a distinct possibility. Stuart had to walk with sticks,
and he was told some time after he had signed up to do the
race that he wouldn't be allowed to complete the two legs
that would take place in the dangerous Southern Ocean. It
was a big blow for someone who had been involved from
the very beginning, and had worked hard on fundraising
for the expedition. Everyone knew, though, what a media

storm there would be if something terrible happened to one of our crew, and I think we all understood how careful the organizers had to be.

Greg Williams used to own a trucking business. All that ended, however, when, at 26, he lost his right leg as a result of two trucks colliding. Needing to find something to take his mind off his terrible injury, Greg took up sailing, and even started teaching the skills to blind people.

Richard Horton-Fawkes was the oldest member of the crew. He came from a family of sailors, but at 25 was diagnosed with glaucoma; by the time he joined the crew of *Time and Tide* he had practically no vision in his left eye and only 25 per cent vision in his right. Richard had sailed with crews half made up of the partially sighted, but never with an all-disabled crew. He was amazing on the helm, and would teach us all a lot about sailing instinctively, by feeling the wind without the use of instruments.

John Rich used to run a TV production company. He had been planning to take part in the 1992–3 Whitbread Round the World Race when he was suddenly diagnosed with stomach cancer. A gruelling period in hospital followed, during which time he had most of his stomach removed. The doctors thought he would die; to their astonishment he walked out with the all-clear. His brush with death made him want to do something challenging in his life.

Carolyn Davies had no hearing in her left ear and only very little in her right – the result of viral pneumonia she contracted when she was just 2 years old. She was able to hear her own voice, and as a result her speech was fairly clear. But for purposes of communication she relied on her ability to lip-read. Carolyn was one of the least experienced sailors – when she signed up she knew nothing about sailing – but she more than made up for it in enthusiasm and strength of character.

Carolyn was not the only deaf crew member. Paul Hebblethwaite, a joiner from York, had hearing loss that was even more profound than hers, and as a result his speech was a lot less understandable. A few of the crew tried to learn sign language in order to communicate with him, but none of them progressed very well, and so it was down to Paul to lip-read and, failing that, Carolyn to sign with him when we needed to converse. Paul was a distinctive-looking guy – with his long, blond hair and splendid moustache, he picked up the nickname 'the Viking'. The Viking had some sailing experience, but he had never gone deep-ocean sailing and was looking forward to the challenge.

In fact, having two deaf members on the crew was not quite the hindrance it might at first appear to be. Certainly it was difficult at night when they were unable to see well enough to lip-read. But during the day it was different. When a sailing boat is travelling at full pelt, the screaming noise of the wind in the sails can be deafening. So a lot of communication is done through hand gestures and by the team working as one organic whole, and being deaf is not a huge obstacle to this; on the contrary, it meant we were able to mouth instructions to them, and they would be able to understand us perhaps better than someone who could hear.

David Tait was a financial trader in the City of London, a man for whom the constant pressure of work meant having a fabulous salary and almost no time to spend it. A year sailing round the world would truly be a sea change for somebody used to that kind of environment. David was severely asthmatic, and had been since he was a young boy. It meant that he didn't *appear* as disabled as the rest of us, and in the lead-up to the race he came under fire from a number of journalists who found his inclusion on a boat supposedly manned only by disabled sailors to be pushing the definition of what it meant to have a disability. They were wrong, as anybody will know who has ever been round somebody having an asthma attack. In terms of awareness-raising, David was just as important as the rest of us – there are, after all, far more asthmatics than amputees – and he was an invaluable part of the crew.

Liz Tring, like Stuart Boreham, suffered from cerebral palsy. Although she had the full complement of limbs, her illness left her very weak and made walking almost as much of a difficulty as it was for the amputees on the boat. Her balance and coordination were compromised, and even the smallest movement was difficult and required the greatest concentration.

Dave Hodder had been born with one leg shorter than the other. Consequently his spine was curved and his heel crooked, which caused him excruciating pain that meant he was only able to stay in bed for four or five hours at a stretch. In many ways Dave had never really thought of himself as being disabled, but our illnesses are all relative and there is no doubt that the chronic back problems he suffered had a detrimental effect on his life.

Our final core crew member was Lesley Bowden. She was a Macmillan nurse who had suffered and survived ovarian cancer at the age of 38, but whose second husband had died from cancer himself. Her son Simon had signed up as a crew member on one of the other boats in the race. When a previous participant on *Time and Tide* who had nursing qualifications pulled out of the race, Simon suggested to his mum that she might consider it. It was crucial that our boat had somebody with medical expertise, for obvious reasons, and Lesley's knowledge would prove to be invaluable. In a lot of ways she was one of the most important members of the crew.

Of the fourteen who started, eight of us completed the race. There would be other crew members who would join us at different times, and who would leave for a variety of reasons. And while our crew may have all had the common denominator of disability, they were a diverse bunch. Nobody was under any illusions about how difficult the race was going to be. To circumnavigate the globe the wrong way round, sailing through some of the most treacherous seas in the world, is extremely difficult at the best of times. We would have to cope with all the challenges with which any large crew confined on a small boat would be presented. The fact that we were disabled didn't mean we wouldn't be subject to the same personality clashes and inter-crew strains that any such team could expect to experience. Over the next few months everybody's character would be laid bare, and this group of people who had been thrust together would not always get on. The winds would not quell and the seas would not calm just because we had extra problems to overcome. We would have to battle against loneliness, fear and all the other emotions that anybody attempting this task would experience.

But there was no getting away from the fact that we had extra difficulties to deal with, me as much as anybody. I was out to show that my injuries didn't have to stop me doing things that an able-bodied person could do, but I couldn't pretend that my legs would not be a profound hindrance. I knew I could look forward to times when the pain would be very bad indeed, when the sores and infections to which I was prone would be as bad as they had ever been. I knew that it was in those times that I would miss Sheila and the children the most. That I would miss home. I knew there would be moments when the psychological battle would be as tough as the physical one.

Chapter Eleven

The Lonely Sea
and the Sky

On 29 September 1996 the fourteen crew members of
Time and Tide, along with the crews of the other
boats in the race, met in Ocean Village, Southampton,
ready for the first leg of the race which would take us
5,300 miles south-west across the Atlantic to Rio de
Janeiro.

Those of us with families had them with us, and we
had a farewell breakfast together. It was an emotional
moment. As I hugged the children I couldn't help but
wonder how different they would be when I saw them
next. The ten months of the race stretched in front of us
like a lifetime, and saying goodbye to them that morning
was one of the hardest things I've ever done. There were
tears and hugs, promises and doubts. It all seemed so
unreal.

Our goodbyes couldn't last for ever. The crew members
were anxious – some of them eager to set off, others

wondering what they'd got themselves into. The weather forecast for that day was extremely poor, and to make things worse our ship's generator broke before we even hoisted sail. If it stayed broken, it wouldn't stop us sailing, but it would mean no power or fresh water all the way to Rio. Chris Ogg had to work hard with an engineer to get it working and thankfully they managed it. But it didn't look as though we were going to be eased into this thing gently.

The opening of the race was a baptism of fire. That day there were force seven or eight gales in the Solent, and the conditions were absolutely horrendous. I had family watching from the beach. And Sheila, the kids, and their grandparents came out on a little ferry to see us off, and were buffeted around as badly as anyone. We barely had the chance to wave goodbye to them as the ocean spray crashed over our boat and into our faces. The wind howled, our ears were filled with the roar of the elements and of the press helicopters following us overhead, and visibility was poor. I discovered, rather alarmingly, that I had a tendency towards seasickness – not a great feeling when you know it's forty days to Rio. The seasickness happily subsided after a couple of days, during which time I frequently had to empty the contents of my stomach, even when on the helm, where I just had to let the rain and spray wash it away. Not a nice feeling at all.

We pushed out to the west. Our families soon disappeared into the distance, and so did land. Before long we were surrounded by a sight we'd have to get very used to:

the ocean – forbidding, grey, and angry – the sky, and nothing else.

The sun hadn't set on our first day's sailing before we sustained our first injury. Our skipper James was at the helm when we slammed through a massive wave. As the huge wheel spun out of control, James fell and caught his hand between it and the floor. It was broken. At the same time someone was violently seasick, spattering the poor skipper, who had to wait for another wave to crash over him before he was cleaned off. Lesley Bowden put his hand in a splint and instructed him to rest it. But it's difficult to rest your hand when there's more than 5,000 miles of sea between you and the next port of call. James would just have to grin and bear it. I also cut my hand quite badly at the start of the race, and had to be patched up by Lesley, but it wasn't nearly so bad as James's mishap.

When you're racing long distance you sail round the clock. This means you need a watch system, whereby half the crew rest while the other half sail. Some crews might split themselves into three watches, but because of our weaknesses we decided to split into two so that we could have more hands on deck at any one time. We weighed up different watch systems, to see which would work best for us. In the end we decided on a three-hours-on, three-hours-off system during the night, and a four-hours-on, four-hours-off system during the day. We decided that was long enough to be up on deck and working, and just long enough to give us time to catch some much-needed sleep in between, as well as do all the other things you needed to do – see to your personal hygiene, eat, unwind with a book, or listen to some music. Because of the nature of our crew, however, it didn't always quite work like that.

There are lots of jobs on a yacht. For example, when you have to tack, you need several people on the winches, letting off or pulling in the ropes that control the sails, as well as somebody on the helm. It's strenuous, physical work, but doesn't necessarily need a lot of leg strength, so our disabled crew was able to deal with it. A much bigger challenge was changing the sails.

A big yacht like *Time and Tide* typically carries a number of different-sized sails. Each member of the Global Challenge fleet was identical, and so carried twelve sails: a mainsail, a trysail, four headsails, two staysails, and four spinnakers. That's a lot of material to handle. As the winds increase in strength, you put a smaller sail on, otherwise you'd end up leaning too far sideways in the water and losing power; as the winds drop, you put on a larger sail to catch more wind. These sails are incredibly heavy: you couldn't just send a single person down below to get a new sail, because it took about four people to carry it. The business of manhandling it out of the sail store, through the hatch and then down to the back of the boat, before taking it forward along the deck to the bow, was strenuous enough for an able-bodied crew; for us it was even more of a task. Only a certain number of us were able to do jobs like that. It meant that even if we were off-watch and supposed to be sleeping, if a sail-change needed to be done, we would all have to get up and get working. For this reason the stronger crew members, of whom I was one, had our sleep broken up a lot and got much less downtime, which took its toll.

Additionally, given the lack of experience of some of the crew, there were only a few of us who could helm – especially now that the skipper had broken his hand and couldn't take the wheel. I was one of them, but I was also a watch leader, and when I wasn't helming I had to take care of the various jobs on the foredeck. And because not many people wanted to go up and down the mast, I was involved with the rig. My parachute-rigging experience meant I was also in charge of sail repair and maintenance. Every time a sail ripped, which seemed to happen quite often with the spinnakers, it was my job to organize a repair and fix it. There wasn't really a part of the boat, from the top of the mast to the bottom of the bilge, that I didn't have to deal with at some stage in the voyage, and in addition to all this were the cooking and cleaning rotas.

That's not to say I was the only busy one. Far from it. There was a lot going on. The moment you came on watch you'd do a handover, finding out from the previous watch leader what had been going on over the previous three or four hours, before looking at the log and the charts and acquainting yourself with the ship's bearing. We would perform all the checks that needed to be done during the daytime watches, and clean the boat scrupulously. With so many people in such a confined space, you really don't want any more germs hanging around than you can help. The ship's generator needed to be maintained, as did the water-maker. All this in addition to the actual sailing of the boat – the trimming of the sails and the main business of trying to get to our destination as quickly as possible.

Mariners have always referred to their boats as 'she' rather than 'it' – the implication being that they are living, breathing things. A vessel is constantly being moved by the immense forces of the sea and the wind: ropes and sails are chafing, screws are unscrewing themselves, nuts are becoming undone and things fall apart behind your back. Consequently there is a constant maintenance programme going on, a perpetual list of elements that need to be checked and tightened and fixed. On a boat, there's never nothing to do. And even when you weren't required on deck, and were having your downtime, it was very difficult to relax. A boat is constantly in motion, so you're always wedged in somewhere, holding on, tense even when you don't realize it.

As skipper and First Mate, James Hatfield and Chris Ogg perhaps bore the greatest brunt of the lack of sleep we all experienced. A little over a week after we'd set sail, I wrote in my diary:

I stuck my head into the nav station. James was there, I thought awake. I asked for his opinion on the sail trim. He came on foredeck, gave it and went down again. After that he made coffee with mashed potato mix instead of milk powder. I didn't realize it, but he was just about walking in his sleep.

As time passed we grew used to the disruptive nature of our watch system. I even came to quite enjoy the intense bouts of excitement interspersed with brief stretches of respite, but there's no denying that those first few days were difficult.

Each boat carried, on that first leg, sufficient food for 2,000 meals. It sounds a lot, but when you're feeding fourteen people three times a day for a month, it soon adds up. Circumstances dictated, however, that the meals would be pretty basic. Fresh food was at a premium, so the majority of what we ate on board was dried or preserved. Our stores contained big slabs of chocolate, which were rationed in a wartime fashion so that each crew member received three or four squares a day. We tended to keep this for the night-time watch: you can often do with a bit of comfort at midnight on a rolling ship. It didn't take long, though, for chocolate to become currency: 'If you clean the toilet for me tomorrow, I'll give you my chocolate ration.' As the race progressed, and our ennui with the food grew worse, we found ourselves spending all our time on watch talking about our favourite meals and how we would cook them. On the first leg I became obsessed with the idea of McDonald's. Of course, when I finally sank my teeth into a Big Mac in Rio, it was nothing like as good as it had been in my head. Being alone at sea can play little tricks with your mind.

In addition to all the dried food and chocolate, we'd brought with us a store of wine and beer. Clearly, however, getting drunk on board wasn't an option. We couldn't just decide that every Friday night we'd all have a few beers, because the boat sailed twenty-four hours a day and we all needed to be capable of managing it. Instead we decided to have a 'happy hour' once a day, when we could all have a single drink – half a glass of wine or a drop of beer. It was a tiny amount – enough to make you want a little bit more, but not enough to relax you after a hard day. With fourteen crew, however, the number of bottles added up. It was a huge amount of weight to be carrying, for just a mouthful of wine a day. So after the first leg we cancelled our happy hour and decided not to bother carrying alcohol any more. It just didn't seem worth it, but it did make us look forward to our stopovers all the more.

Our route to Rio took us in a straight line diagonally across the Atlantic and over the equator. The bad weather that had accompanied us out of Southampton lasted for about a week, and it shook everybody up. But after that rough start the sun came out; and as we sailed further south towards the equator, the weather became increasingly pleasant and we were able to start enjoying the voyage, rather than just worrying all the time about seasickness and the brutal business of keeping the boat on course and upright in rough seas. The sailing became good, and for a while we made impressive time.

It couldn't last for ever. Not on this leg. As we got close to the equator we entered the doldrums. This is an area of low pressure caused by the equatorial heat making air rise high into the atmosphere and travel north or south. As a result, there are few prevailing winds and it's common for ships to become becalmed. We were stuck in the doldrums for a number of days. It's about the most frustrating thing that can happen on a yacht. You can deal with lots of wind by changing the sails; when there's no wind at all, there's nothing you can do. In the doldrums you also have to contend with heat exhaustion and exposure to the sun.

At times like that you just have to be positive and make the most of things. As we bobbed around in the doldrums, a few of the guys took the opportunity to have a swim in the sea. It wasn't something you'd ever normally do when you're racing, but we weren't going anywhere so there seemed no harm in it. I stayed in the boat, but while the others were swimming I saw something approaching in the water: it was a pod of porpoises. I got into the water immediately, thrilled by the thought that we might be able to swim with these dolphin-like creatures. In the end they didn't come closer than about fifty feet, but it was a memorable moment, just the few of us so close to the natural world, miles from any other sign of humans.

I shouted out to the skipper, 'Are you coming in?'

He refused. 'I know what's down there,' he said.

At times you could feel very isolated in the middle of the ocean. Other times you would find yourself in the company of other creatures, and be amazed at their ability to exist out there. One day we were up on deck and found ourselves surrounded by a swarm of the most intensely blue butterflies I'd every seen. I don't know what they were, or how they'd arrived in the middle of the ocean – perhaps they'd been picked up by an updraught somewhere in Africa and blown far out to sea – but there were hundreds of them, all over the place, on deck, below deck, and even down the back of our clothes.

The doldrums were frustrating, but they gave us a little time for reflection. There's something moving about spending so much time with the ocean: there's just you, and the sea, and the birds, and the fish. You're at one with nature and it's a magical experience. And one of the beauties of such a long race is the ample chances you get to sail at night. There's no artificial light in the middle of the sea, so the stars and planets form the most amazing, glowing canopy that stretches down like a dome to the horizon. It's like being in a planetarium, only a thousand times more breathtaking.

There is a seagoing tradition that when a sailor passes over the equator for the first time, he or she should pay homage to Neptune for his kindness and protection. The ceremony involves the skipper, dressed as Neptune, and any others who have passed this way before, pouring a horrible concoction of cold porridge and whatever else he can find over the heads of the newly initiated. When we sailed over the equator, those of us for whom it was the first time were given this honour.

Gradually the wind picked up a bit and we started moving with more speed towards Rio. The tempo on the boat resumed its previous level, and just as before I found myself required to work at any hour of the day on all the different parts of the boat. I wrote in my log that, 'If this was a job, I'd have left by now.' But in truth I don't remember feeling especially resentful that I was working hard. On the contrary, I think I relished the opportunity to pull my weight, to prove that I could do whatever needed doing, to handle whatever the sea threw at me. In a situation like that, it's hard to pace yourself properly, even when you know you should. If something needs to be done on a boat, it generally can't wait, no matter how grotty the crew members might be feeling. For me, and for the others on *Time and Tide*, that was all part of the challenge. It might be a cliché, but it's true that the more you put into such an endeavour, the more you get out.

As usual, though, I probably pushed myself too far. We were a week out of Rio when I developed an abscess in my right knee and severe bruising on my foot. I wrote in my log: 'You know me – I've overdone it again. Here I am, foot up with an ice pack on. Stump sore, big bruise on side of foot. I just don't know when to stop.'

But I had to stop. With my leg in such a bad state, I had to take a back seat for the final week while the others – many of whom were also feeling the physical strain of the race – brought *Time and Tide* into the shadow of the statue of Christ the Redeemer, and the carnival town of Rio. Ours was the last boat to finish the leg, coming in just three and a half hours after our nearest competitor. Even so, it had been a great achievement: we had shown that, despite our disabilities, we could handle a boat with the same level of aptitude as our able-bodied competitors. And that felt good. I wrote in my log:

This leg has had its ups and downs. A big up being watch leader, and taking the helm and being in control and responsible for all on board. To helm *Time and Tide* across the Atlantic you feel part of her – you feel you really are personally racing to Rio. I've been from the top of the mast to the bottom of the bilge, from bow to stern, and I've even swum alongside. I've been alive and bouncing with energy then laid up, my legs having let me down. Rio is just around the corner and with it proper rest, real food, maybe a drink or two – then the race starts for real.

It was indeed a fabulous moment when we crossed the finish line on a bright Brazilian morning, to be handed a bottle of champagne by a waiting news crew and to celebrate what we'd just achieved. We all knew, however, that Southampton to Rio was just the warm-up leg. The weather had been relatively clement, the seas relatively calm. It had been nothing like the kind of sailing we could expect to encounter next.

We stopped in Rio for just under a month. Time to recuperate, prepare ourselves for the next leg, and, crucially, give our boat some TLC. The sails for all the boats in the race had been supplied by a company called Hood, and they'd sent one of their reps out to check them all for any problems while we were at anchor in Rio. The rep was on our boat one afternoon when he started feeling unwell. The next morning we found out that he'd died in the night – he had contracted meningitis before he came out to Rio. A tragedy for him and his family, and one that left us all feeling deeply shocked. It also meant that, because of the incubation period of the disease, our departure had to be delayed for ten days, with all of us wondering if we'd caught it.

We had to do a lot of corporate hospitality, and attended some great parties, in order to raise the profile of the race; but we also got the chance to explore Rio. It was a fantastic place, but an eye-opening one: as we'd approached the harbour we'd heard one of the other boats announcing over the radio that they'd seen a body floating in the water. Not something you'd really expect to see off the Isle of Wight. And when one of our crew, John Rich, went into town to do some sightseeing, he came back with a white face and a wild look in his eyes. 'Someone just got shot in front of me,' he told us all. 'I think they died.' I didn't see anything quite that dramatic, but after a few of us had been to see a local football derby in the massive Olympic stadium, we were just about to pile into a taxi when someone a few feet away from us shot another man in the thigh. The taxi driver yelled at us to get in – we were more than happy to do what he said – and sped off. The uniformed police all carried a sidearm, but they also had a gun in a shoulder holster or stuck down the back of their belt. This was clearly a place where we had to be careful.

One of the bars we used to frequent, a street back from the touristy glare of the Copacabana Beach, was Ronnie Biggs's local, and although we never actually saw him we enjoyed seeing some of the real Rio, rather than the tourist façade. We'd been told not to dress up when we were off the beaten track, so I took to removing my watch and secreting my wedding ring inside my wallet.

One evening the crew went to a local Brazilian restaurant in our team T-shirts and sailing trousers. These trousers didn't have very adequate pockets, so your wallet was forever peeping out over the top. We had a good night, with lots of wine and good food – much needed after the less than abundant rations on board *Time and Tide* – and we left the restaurant in a fairly merry state. We were heading back to the hotel along the seafront when two women came up to me. One of them put her arm round my shoulder, while the other one started gabbling away with a big smile. It was only after a few moments, as I looked more closely at their faces, that I realized the truth: these weren't women, they were blokes dressed up as women. And then, within seconds, my new friends had gone. They had just melted away into the crowd when my hand went down to the pocket of my sailing trousers to find … no wallet. And that meant no wedding ring. I'd just been robbed by two transvestite pickpockets – but then I suppose I *had* embarked on this voyage in search of new experiences!

I was shocked by the abruptness of the dividing line between rich and poor in Rio. There seemed to be no middle ground – you were either a millionaire or you were grindingly poor. Our hotel – a very unprepossessing place because of the difficulty the charity had raising money – was just on Copacabana Beach, and my room was on the side of the building. If I stood on my balcony and looked to the left, I could see all the smiley, happy people enjoying the beach and going up and down on rollerblades; if I looked to my right, I could see nothing but the shanty towns and impoverished underbelly of Rio: cardboard houses and even, just outside my window, a family living in the street. It was a reminder that there's always someone worse off than you.

We took a cable car up to the Sugarloaf Mountain, from where we could look out over our yacht, lying at anchor in the bay below, and up to the huge statue of Christ. We also managed to get out of Rio to see a bit more of Brazil. Nigel, Paul and I hired a very basic, locally made VW Golf and headed out through the dangerous suburbs of the city. Our destination was a spa town, a couple of days' drive away, that had been built by Swiss colonists a century or so ago. Our route took us along the coast, where we stayed overnight in a little sailing club, but the further we got from Rio, the worse the road became. It changed from a big dual carriageway, into a single-lane road, into a track. The track got more and more winding, and hillier and hillier, until it was just a mud path with sheer cliffs down one side. We passed cows herded by *gauchos*, and the terrain became wilder and more forbidding. Finally we found ourselves out in the jungle in our little car – it was like travelling through a mountainous rainforest, a far cry from anything I'd ever experienced before, and not really what I'd imagined when I signed up for a round-the-world yacht race.

The first leg of the Global Challenge had been eventful, not just in terms of the sailing, but also in terms of the crew members' interactions. I felt personally that I'd managed to get on OK with everybody – not easy in such confined quarters and under such stressful conditions. And it had been significant that, when we got into port, rather than all bomb-bursting in different directions, mostly we continued to stick together as a tight-knit unit. The strains of the first leg had, however, left their mark on certain members of the crew. Richard, Dave and Greg decided for various reasons that they wanted to leave the boat. This, in addition to the fact that Stuart would not be rejoining us until Leg 5 as he was deemed medically unfit to tackle the Southern Ocean, meant that we were going to lose a lot of sailing experience and a lot of strength. And this we could ill afford to do as we embarked upon the most dangerous part of the voyage.

Nobody undertakes to sail the Southern Ocean lightly. It's impossible to train for this kind of sailing, because the kind of seas we were going to encounter simply don't exist anywhere else in the world. This would be one of the most demanding things any of us would ever do, and I include the able-bodied crews in that as well as the crew of *Time and Tide*. There would be no calm days, sunshine, and swimming with porpoises; just a constant battering from the sea and the elements. Those of us who were about to sail the second leg of the BT Global Challenge had some idea of what we were in for, and it would be wrong to say there weren't some anxieties among the crew about what the next few weeks held.

We took encouragement from wherever we could get it. The same boats that we were sailing had survived the Southern Ocean four years earlier during the British Steel Challenge, so we knew they should stand up to those dangerous seas. And having successfully completed the first leg, and all the training that went before it, we had some confidence in our abilities.

We were, however, four men down when we took into account that Stuart wasn't allowed to sail the Southern Ocean. These berths needed filling, otherwise it would be even more difficult to handle the boat on this dangerous leg of the race. We wouldn't be able to manage with less strength, or less seamanship. Fortunately the charity back in the UK had been hard at work, and four new members of the *Time and Tide* crew joined us in Rio. One of them was a face from my past.

When I was in the Queen Elizabeth after the Warren-point bombings, and my mum was staying in the Red Cross accommodation, another guy was in the hospital at the same time and our parents shared a flat. His name was Brendan West. He was a similar age to me and had a similar background. He'd been serving with the Royal

Electrical and Mechanical Engineers in Germany when a hit-and-run driver had knocked him over and then he was hit by the car behind. Brendan was lucky not to be killed, but he sustained terrible damage to his body: his chest was crushed and he had to have a tracheotomy; he lost the lower part of his left leg – it was amputated through the knee – and almost lost his other leg, which was held together by two steel pins. It was a small community in the hospital and we soon became friends, going on to spend some time together at the rehabilitation centre in Chessington. But after that, Brendan had left the Army to retrain as a computer engineer and I'd gone back to the Parachute Regiment. We lost touch as our lives took us on different paths, but our parents had always kept in contact.

Brendan had been invited by a colleague to see the start of the BT Global Challenge race in Southampton, and even then had been interested in the concept of *Time and Tide*, despite having no sailing experience at all. When he saw in one of the newspapers that were following our progress that we were suddenly short of crew members, he applied for a place. Three days after he'd handed in his application form, he was accepted. So it was that I met up with Brendan after nearly twenty years, and it marked the start of a renewed friendship that would last until this day.

In addition to Brendan, we still had three other berths to fill. Mike Austin was a British Airways 747 pilot by profession, and also had quite a lot of sailing experience. Three years before the race he'd been diagnosed with leukaemia, but that hadn't stopped him from sailing 3,000 miles even while he was undergoing chemotherapy. It sounded like madness, but as Mike pointed out to me, when your immune system is struggling, as it does with chemotherapy, the ocean's not a bad place to be as there are far fewer germ-carrying people out on the water.

The departure of Richard Horton-Fawkes meant that our third newcomer, John Anderson, was now the oldest member of the crew. John had undergone a hip-replacement operation just a year previously, and he too had been alerted to our need for crew members by the publicity in the press back home. Our final replacement member was Carol Sear, a 35-year-old accountant with a little more sailing experience than Brendan, but not much. She had restricted movement in one arm as a result of a motorcycling accident when she was a teenager.

All in all, our new crew members were a friendly, enthusiastic bunch, two of whom also brought with them a good deal of sailing experience. We would need it for Leg 2, and it was with a mixture of trepidation and excitement that we set sail once more on *Time and Tide*, knowing that the next time our feet hit dry land we would be in Wellington, New Zealand.

Chapter Twelve

The Southern Ocean

Sending a disabled crew into the Southern Ocean was controversial. Back home in the sailing community, a number of people questioned whether this was something responsible race organizers should really be doing. We knew that if we were to be considered the equal of the able-bodied crews, we would have to dig deep, but I think the fact that certain people had doubts about our chances of success made us even more determined to succeed.

In racing terms we started badly – the last of all the boats to cross the starting line. But we'd only been in the water for a short while when *Time and Tide* found a bright breeze and we quickly overtook half the others. You could immediately feel the morale on the yacht lift as we all realized that we were doing what we set out to do: proving that we had it in us to match or even better the achievements of our able-bodied competitors.

Before we knew it, we were leading the fleet. And while we didn't maintain our first position for more than a couple of days, we remained frontrunners for a good while, to the delight of everyone who was following us back home. We enjoyed ourselves as we sped down the coast of South America, past the Falkland Islands – a poignant moment for any former member of the Parachute Regiment. I'd have liked to stop off there, to visit where my Army mates saw action. But this was a race, not a sightseeing tour, so we sped past and continued down towards Cape Horn, the southern tip of Chile.

Cape Horn is legendary, and feared by sailors. The need to navigate it for commercial purposes was greatly reduced in 1914 by the opening of the Panama Canal. Round-the-world yacht races, however, always go round the Horn, and it's accepted as being one of the toughest routes a boat can sail. The winds are strong, the waves are large, and icebergs are a constant threat. The number of sailors who, throughout history, have lost their lives rounding Cape Horn cannot be counted. Its hazardous sailing conditions are caused by a number of different meteorological phenomena. Strong winds are able to blow uninterrupted round the south of the globe, and they cause correspondingly high waves. And there are dangers you can't see: it is here that the South American continental shelf changes the depth of the sea from 13,000 to 600 feet, a dramatic decrease that causes ferocious currents and unpredictable rogue waves.

Heading westward round the Horn has always been the most difficult way of navigating it. The temperature changed gradually as we headed south from Rio. It is from the southern tip of Chile that tourist boats to Antarctica depart, and the closer we grew to those icy climes, the more chilling the air and the water became. And as we prepared to turn round the Horn, suddenly to be faced with the full reality of these natural phenomena, the weather report came in. The conditions round the Horn were expected to be particularly cruel. James Hatfield decided to continue further south before heading westward so that we avoided the worst of that weather. It was a slower route, but a slightly safer one, and although I was disappointed not to get Cape Horn in my sights, I could see the wisdom of our skipper's decision.

The Southern Ocean is characterized by the most enormous waves any sea can throw at you, some of them sixty feet high. It reminded me of a bleak, hilly landscape, only these aren't hills, they're waves. You sail up and over them, and then when you're in the trough you're entirely surrounded by mammoth walls of water. You learn to identify different types of wave. When they are rolling, with rounded peaks, it's not too bad; when you see the crests grow sharper and more pointy, things can become decidedly hairy. If you're forced to go over a very high wave with a small top, the stern of the boat comes out of the water, and so does the rudder: all of a sudden you have no steerage on the boat, a sail full of wind and no control on the wheel. If it weren't for the fact that under these conditions every member of the crew is constantly hooked onto the boat, you could easily end up in the water. Even so, there's still a fear that the boat might be put on its side, or rolled. This does sometimes happen, but as long as the keel – which acts as an enormous pendulum – doesn't become detached from the hull, the boat will right itself. It can cause a lot of damage, though, especially to the people inside who are thrown about, so when you sleep you have to strap yourself into your bunk. When you're at the helm and everyone's relying on you, the moment when you cross the sharp crest of a sixty-foot wave and realize you're not in control of the boat is a chilling one.

Sometimes you reach the crest of a wave and, rather than having a similar incline to sail down, you're faced with a vertical drop: the boat plummets back down into the next trough with nothing underneath it. Sometimes a wave will crash over the boat that is so large it knocks your feet from under you, and you're only saved from landing in the drink by clinging to the wheel and relying on the safety line that attaches you to the boat. In high winds and rolling seas such as these, you *can* sail very sensibly, with a small amount of sail. But we were racing, so we had to push things as far as we could – both in terms of what the boat could withstand and what *we* could withstand. It's up to the skipper to decide how fast to go in circumstances like that, and I think some of us felt we could have been less reserved in the Southern Ocean. But I can understand how, given the nature of our crew, James might have wanted to err on the side of caution.

Nevertheless, there were still moments on the second leg when I personally got into difficulty. The technique of sailing over the massive waves of that ocean is to approach the steep inclines at an angle. The wind is different in the troughs from on the peaks, and with all the forces bombarding the boat, you need to concentrate very hard and stay focused on controlling your vessel, but also on treating it as kindly as you can. These angled approaches are less harsh on the boat. I was helming one day in such conditions, when I sailed too close to the wind. I momentarily lost control, and the wind passed to the other side of the sail. This is called a tack, and normally when it happens you have the crew set to change the positions of the sails accordingly. An unintended tack, however, can be dangerous, especially in seas like that, but thankfully not too difficult to rectify. The skipper was there immediately, shouting orders, and all hands were called on deck. Sails were tacked across the boat and winched in tight; lines were tidied away and we sailed on. But it was hard work in the middle of these terrible waves.

The boats we were sailing were amazing, and specifically designed to handle the Southern Ocean. On occasion, though, they failed us. The main sail had reinforcing batons, great rods that are sandwiched onto the sail to give it some structure and stability. At one stage these rods snapped, so the whole main sail had to come down. In big seas, the main sail gives you a certain amount of stability; when it comes down you lose that stability and are more at the mercy of the elements. I was on the low side of the yacht with most of the sail down, replacing the baton, when a huge, freak wave engulfed us. It picked me up and carried me back the entire length of the boat to the end of the jackstay, where my safety line snapped taut with a jolt. I seemed to have water in every orifice, and I remember seeing the skipper at the helm looking down at me from quite a height because of the angle at which the boat was set.

One of our sponsors was Henri Lloyd, who make foul-weather clothing for yachtsmen. The company had provided us all with a full layering system to wear in these fierce seas. There was a base layer and two layers of warm, fleecy clothes, then an outer layer of protective waterproofs. For the first leg of the race, most of this had been kept in deep storage, but the further south we sailed, the more layers we started wearing. Now that we were in the Southern Ocean, we had to wear the full gear. It grew perishingly cold, and we knew that we were approaching the region where we could easily encounter an iceberg. We had been taught that the icebergs themselves were not the greatest problem – they were big enough to see and navigate around, and unlike in the days of the *Titanic* we had the advantage of radar and constant updates from the race organizers to warn us of any large obstacles in our way.

More worrying than the icebergs were the 'growlers'. These are big lumps of ice that have broken away from melting icebergs, and they're like an ice cube in your gin and tonic: they have flat tops and they float just below the surface of the water. You'd be lucky to see them during the day, and at night you haven't got a chance. If you're doing ten or twelve knots and you hit one of these lumps of ice, you can do a lot of damage to the boat; and because they're underwater you can't see them on the radar any better than you can with your eyes.

Our boats were designed with growlers in mind and had the benefit of two crash bulkheads. These were effectively steel walls that protected the bow of the boat, meaning that if we did hit an obstacle, it would have to puncture two of these walls before any water started entering the main part of the vessel. We had the same system at the back. A collision would still mangle the boat quite nicely, but hopefully we wouldn't sink.

It wasn't just ice we had to worry about colliding with. Lots of boats have been sunk after collisions with whales; trees and driftwood float around the seas; and sometimes cargo ships sail with big containers piled so high that these topple off in strong winds and rough seas, and then, sitting just below the water like growlers, they bob around as an alarming danger to shipping. Hitting a large metal container at twelve knots won't do the boat much good at all.

I'd learned on the first leg about the boat being a living, moving thing, requiring daily attention and constant care. The more severe conditions of the Southern Ocean – the high winds and the pounding of the waves – made us increasingly aware of this. Taking care of the vessel wasn't made any easier by the fact that our time on deck was limited because of the cold. Even with all the foul-weather gear and goggles on, you couldn't helm for much longer than half an hour. After this time the cold and the wet would get to you, as would the exhausting effort of controlling the wheel in such heavy seas. Your limbs would go numb from the cold. We wore thick mountain-eering gloves with fleece inside; sometimes we had neoprene gloves too. The rain and the spray would still get through them, so you grew used to having constantly wet hands. Much of my time on deck was spent with my fingers pointing skywards to stop the rain and spray drip-ping down my clothes and into my gloves, which were always soaking. The layers protected your fingers from the biting chill of the wind, but there are many jobs on a boat that you simply can't perform with gloves on – undo-ing shackles, fixing sails, clipping your harness to the safety lines on the boat so you don't get flung into the sea.

Sailing the Southern Ocean was, for me, many things: exhilarating, fun, challenging. It could also be incredibly gruelling. At one point I chipped the bone in my elbow and developed a bursitis – a big, inflamed lump on my arm. It looked worse than it felt, but the relentless weeks of sailing in conditions like these could wear you down. Although half of me thrived on the excitement and the adventure, it was inevitable, I suppose, that we would all have moments of difficulty as the sea threw everything it had at us. On 13 December I wrote in my log:

No real rest for more than two or three hours at a time, cold, and everything damp – sleeping bag, pillow etc. The clothes you wear on deck are drenched by waves and rain. It is very difficult for me to get my boot off my left leg, so I'll just leave it in my sea boot, I suppose. The noise is loud and constant – wind and seas, and the crash as we fall from a wave is indescribable. I use ear plugs and eye patches to help me sleep but am so run down I would probably sleep anyway. There is heating but it's not very good. One cabin is like a sauna; the rest cold and damp. I feel so fed up I could cry. I wish I was at home with the family. I'm in the middle of the biggest wilderness on earth and not coping very well.

In fact I think I was coping better than I sounded, and I tried to deal with the psychological and physical strains of being on the boat by pushing myself to work harder.

And it's not as if it was all misery. We all knew that this leg of the race wouldn't last for ever, that in a few weeks we would be sailing into safe harbour in Wellington. And despite its ferocity, the sea has its own kind of wild beauty. About three weeks into the leg we caught our only glimpse of an iceberg. It was about four miles away, and appeared to bob above and below the peaks and troughs of the sea. But even from a distance, it was a magnificent sight. Occasionally we would spot an albatross. They start as just a speck in the distance that you can't really identify; they approach you without a beat of their wings, gliding overhead. Sometimes the birds' wing tips slice through the water as they fly round the boat, and before you know it they're away and over the horizon. You can't look at them without feeling privileged. And there is a certain magnificence to the sight of the boiling skies, the lashing rain and the angry sea. Miles from land, feeling like a pinprick in the vast expanse of ocean, you see a side of the world that few people ever witness, and it's hard not to feel humbled.

My legs suffered. The abscess on my foot returned, and my stump grew incredibly sore and infected. Just before Christmas, the leather strap that held my false leg to my body broke. It made movement that bit more difficult, but I dealt with it the only way I knew how: by pushing myself to work harder for the team. Besides, other people had to suffer much worse injuries than me during that second leg of the race.

The minimum number of people we could have on deck was two: one to helm, one to control the main sheet. Brendan was performing this latter duty, sitting on the floor, braced in the safest position. Chris Ogg came out to relieve whoever was helming at the time when a wave hit. Chris was thrown across the deck and landed squarely on Brendan's good knee. It was a nasty thing to happen, but especially nasty for Brendan as he'd had a lot of surgery on that knee back in the Queen Elizabeth Military Hospital after his accident. I was off watch at the time, grabbing some sleep. Brendan woke me up with his blood-curdling screams that were audible even above the noise of the wind.

It was all hands on deck to move Brendan back down below – not an easy task in high winds and high seas. His good leg was strapped to his false one, and we constructed a makeshift slide out of spare sails to get him down into the hull of the boat, where we cut away the clothing round his knee. It was badly swollen, and even though Brendan insisted that he'd only twisted the joint, it seemed pretty clear that his knee was broken. Lesley made him a splint and gave him painkillers.

Probably the best course of action would have been to airlift Brendan out so that he could get proper medical treatment, especially as we only had enough painkillers to last about six days. But as his life wasn't endangered by his injury, the insurance wouldn't have paid for the airlift. Consequently we had to rendezvous with another of the boats in order to get more medical supplies from them. Painkillers or not, however, Brendan would have to endure another couple of weeks on board with the excruciating pain of a broken knee that was made even worse by the constant jolting of the boat. It was most unpleasant for him, and for all of us who had to comfort him, but he amazed us all by the way he managed to stay cheerful even when the pain was agonizing.

Ours was not the only boat that needed to beg assistance from another member of the fleet. It may have been a race, but when things went wrong we had to be able to help our fellow competitors. The *Concert*, which had done very well in the first leg and had come in third position, had lost half her mast because of the brutal conditions. Her crew had jury-rigged the sails up as best they could but were relying on their back-up engines to finish the leg. For this they needed fuel – we all carried the minimum we needed for the generator – and as we were their nearest vessel it was our duty to meet up with them and share some of ours – an act of benevolence that wouldn't be without risk because if we suffered the same fate as them we'd be scuppered. None of us wanted to leave them struggling, however, so we altered our course so as to meet up. I'll always remember seeing that boat bobbing up and down on the horizon like a cork as we approached – a sudden reminder of how small our vessels were in the vastness of the ocean. We drew up alongside her, threw a line across, and rigged up a pulley system. We were dangerously close to being smashed together. Down in the hull Nigel pumped the emergency water jerrycans full of diesel from our fuel storage system, and in the end we winched over to the *Concert* 100 gallons of diesel, along with a few other bits and bobs. In return they sent over to us all their morphine and painkillers to help with Brendan's injury. It being almost Christmas, Carol had made them a loaf of bread in the shape of a reindeer, and as we drifted away they sang us a Christmas carol.

We all knew that Christmas would be a difficult moment in the race. It fell during one of the toughest legs and it would be now that we missed our families most of all. When Christmas Day came, it brought with it some of the toughest, roughest weather we'd seen: a mighty storm with huge waves that crashed over the boat and hurled us from one end to the other. We had to perform one of the most difficult sail changes of the voyage, and I don't think there was a single one of us who wasn't bruised and exhausted by that day. We made a pretty good stab at being festive, with the nearest thing we could manage to a Christmas dinner and, for a short time at least, a party atmosphere below deck. There were decorations and stockings, and even a special Christmas meal. Someone had to helm the ship while all this was happening, though, and that fell to David Tait and myself. I was more than happy to let the others enjoy their meal as it wasn't in my nature to sit back while other people were working; but it was a bit surreal to peer through the misted window of the cockpit and see the warm glow of the others having a party while all around us it was dark and stormy. David later said that he felt like a character from *A Christmas Carol*, watching all the merriment from the bleakness of outside.

The weather would get even worse before it got better. Four days out of Wellington, reports indicated that we were sailing into the path of Hurricane Fergus. We managed to avoid the worst of it, but we still caught its tail winds, which reached speeds of sixty knots, buffeting the boat like never before and meaning that only the most experienced crew members were allowed to helm. Finally, however, on 2 January 1997, we made it across the finishing line in eleventh place, and into the harbour at

Wellington. We received the most marvellous welcome. Chay Blyth was there, along with all the Global Challenge staff and the crews from the other boats, and 'Simply the Best' was played over the loudspeaker. It was very humbling to be welcomed by other people who had experienced the savage beauty of the Southern Ocean just as we had. We were exhausted, bruised, and in some cases badly injured. But we'd done it, and there was no better feeling than that.

The people of Wellington couldn't have been more welcoming. In Rio the majority didn't really care that there were a few people in big posh yachts down in the bay, but here we had the impression that the New Zealanders were glad we were there. Every boat had its own sponsored pub and restaurant, the town was plastered with BT Global Challenge banners, and as we walked down the street all the locals seemed to know who we were. We felt like movie stars. At least, we would have done if two of our number hadn't had to be admitted to hospital the moment we landed. Brendan, of course, needed have his leg set at once. He was obviously out of the next part of the race, but would join up with us again when we reached Cape Town. John Rich was also in trouble. He had lost more than two stone in weight during the last leg, and his health was compromised. Doctors discovered an infection and told him to pull out of the race. John wasn't happy about it, but he agreed.

I had been particularly looking forward to Wellington. This was the halfway point of the race. The boats needed a thorough going over, so we had a six-week break, and from here I flew back home to the UK for a two-week holiday with the family. To see the children again after so long was like taking a cold drink after weeks in the desert. We holidayed in London, seeing all the sights and just enjoying being together.

Back in New Zealand, I looked up an ex-Army friend who was working in a parachute centre on the South Island. I organized a little trip for about half the guys in the crew, none of whom had done a jump before, to try their hand at skydiving. They all did tandem jumps, strapped to instructors, while I followed them out by myself. Our hosts also gave us a trip round the local vineyards and entertained us with a hospitality that made us feel right at home. After the tribulations of the second leg of the race, it was good to be able to relax and recuperate.

The next leg, from Wellington to Sydney, was known as the Director's Leg. A 1,230-mile sprint across the Tasman Sea – a short hop, really, after what we'd managed before – it was designed to allow sponsors and others who had been involved in the setting-up of the race to join the crews for a short leg. We were joined by Tony Gledhill, one of our sponsors, who had no disability, and a yachting journalist called Malcolm McKeag, who was blind in one eye. Our crew was also bolstered by the arrival of Geoff Morphew, a serious diabetic who would have a lot of difficulty at the start of the race because he got so seasick he was unable to eat or drink.

We completed the leg in a week, and had the pleasure of sailing past the Sydney Opera House and under the bridge into Darling Harbour. We had the good fortune to be put up in the Ritz-Carlton hotel, which was good for body and soul as we prepared for the next leg of the race. It would take us the 6,200 miles to Cape Town and meant another gruelling voyage across the Southern Ocean.

Chapter Thirteen

Sea Change

We all expected the leg from Sydney to Cape Town to be the worst part of the race, so it wasn't a great start when we learned we were losing three crew members. Mike Austin, the BA pilot, had been told by his doctors not to attempt this stage of the race; our diabetic newcomer Geoff Morphew decided that the Southern Ocean would be too much for him and pulled out, promising to rejoin us at Cape Town; and Liz Tring left for her own reasons as well. I couldn't blame anyone for not wanting to continue the race after the strains of the first Southern Ocean leg, but there was no doubt that losing experienced crew members was a blow.

They were replaced by Grahme Rayner, a sergeant in the Australian Army who had lost a leg when he was knocked off his Harley-Davidson. His injury had happened relatively recently, which meant his stump was not yet totally healed and could shrink in his prosthetic leg, so just for fun he'd had a peg-leg made specifically for the race. Clive Dutton, a New Zealander, had lost his right hand in a horrific accident while operating a meat mincer. When the paramedics had arrived, they'd had to free him from the mincer using a drill and amputate the limb there and then. Steve Latter worked in computers and came from Hampshire. Ten years previously he'd had a terrible fall, from a height of forty feet and onto concrete, as a result of which he was suffering a wasting condition of the limbs. Even with these extra members, however, we were still two crew short of full strength. Not ideal for this stage of the race.

Chay Blyth almost didn't allow me to get on the boat either. My foot was bad, my false leg was giving me pain, and while the bursitis on my chipped elbow looked more alarming than it was, the fact that I'd spent as much time as possible before the race wearing a sling meant that now only one of my limbs was uninjured. I'd have been devastated if I hadn't been allowed to continue, but happily I was given the green light and I was determined to make the most of it.

We seemed to be constantly wet travelling from Sydney to Cape Town. Our foul-weather gear was no match for the incessant, stormy seas. Even if our clothes managed to repel the water from outside, changing sails was such strenuous work that we sweated profusely. Our under layers would quickly absorb the moisture from our skin but our outer layers were permanently soaked. There were no washing or drying facilities down below, and since the walls were constantly dripping with condensation, the only way of drying off was to get inside your sleeping bag and let the warmth of your body evaporate the moisture.

As we'd feared, the weather was worse than on our first crossing of the Southern Ocean. I've never been fully able to describe to someone on land what the seas were like – people think you're making it up when you explain how tall the waves were and how the boat would just disappear in the troughs. Several times I was at the helm and a wave would crash over me with such force that I thought the wheel would come away from the boat. And several times I was knocked from my feet and only kept my place at the helm by gripping onto that precarious-feeling wheel for dear life. You took your life in your hands simply brushing your teeth, because one lurch of the boat and you could end up swallowing your toothbrush or taking your eye out. You'd have to strap yourself to your bunk, otherwise when the boat fell off a particularly big wave you'd enter zero gravity and bash into the bunk above you. The boat was constantly at an angle, so nothing was ever flat – to get from one side of the vessel to another was like climbing a hill. And we had to wear goggles on deck, otherwise it would be impossible to see on account of the wind and the salty spray hitting your eyes.

Perhaps the second Southern Ocean leg *should* have been easier than the first. After all, we'd had time to get used to this kind of sailing. But we just experienced storm after storm after storm. Although there were moments when you couldn't help but feel downcast by the relent-lessness of the conditions, I nevertheless thrived on them. In some ways it reminded me of being back at Para depot, working to get my red beret and my wings. There were differences, of course. My legs hurt almost constantly, as it's impossible to sit down and helm a boat under such conditions, but I wasn't going to let that stop me from doing my bit, so I just gritted my teeth and got on with it – with the help of a lot of painkillers. I loved being part of a team where every member was an integral part of making things happen. Predictably, however, this leg of the race was not without its problems.

Paul Hebblethwaite, one of our deaf crew members, was a particularly important part of the team and a watch leader on this leg. We weren't even a day out of Sydney, however, when he had an accident that still makes my eyes water to think about it. He was up on the foredeck in the small hours when an enormous wave crashed over us. It knocked Paul from his feet and sent him hurtling the length of the boat. On any sailing ship there are a number of cleats, which are T-shaped metal fittings to which you fix your ropes, or warps when you're moored in harbour. The wave, having picked Paul up, deposited him on one of these cleats with terrible force. It ripped into the skin of his perineum, the piece of skin between his balls and bum.

Poor Paul howled with pain. But because of his deaf-ness, his speech was impaired and he couldn't explain to anyone what had happened. He just struggled down below, ripped off his foul-weather gear, and pulled down his shorts to show the skipper what had happened. James took one look at the blood that was flowing from him, and immediately called Lesley. Her nursing skills were really tested as she gave Paul a local anaesthetic and stitched him up while several people held him down over the galley table, performing all this as the boat was being tormented by the wind and the waves.

Paul was unbelievably brave. He barely made a sound as he suffered this almost medieval operation, and subsequently was confined to his bunk, where he refused to make a big deal of his injuries. It was all very unpleasant for him, and it meant we were another crew member down. Even when Paul had recovered sufficiently to come back out on deck, he moved gingerly, and who could blame him?

Soon after we left Sydney the seas grew calm for a couple of days, and for that short time we dared to hope that we might have a calm crossing. No such luck. After you've spent a certain amount of time at sea, you start to have a feeling for the sounds and movements your boat makes: interpreting the creaks and the rustles of the sails becomes second nature. It soon became apparent that our short interval of calm wasn't going to last.

And when the storms got up again they were worse than before, sending the boat flying into the air and plunging into the sea. I saw a wind reading on the instruments of seventy-four knots; others said they saw it even higher. The crew members dealt in their own way with the bruising nature of the storms. Some of us revelled in it; others were so paralysed with fear that they could barely come up from below deck. Exhaustion set in, and there were plenty of tears. Even the most experienced sailors started to make mistakes. Because of the terrible conditions, we changed sails as infrequently as possible, keeping the smallest sails on to deal with the very high winds and only changing up to the largest to get up speed when we were sure it was safe. One day during a storm Steve made tea for all the crew but instead of adding milk powder he added custard powder. Interesting taste, but everyone drank it because it was hot.

My false leg didn't fare very well at sea. The leather and tin became encrusted in salt from the spray and started to break down. It was so difficult to peel my drysuit away from my false foot – I'd have people trying to pull away my clothes and invariably hauling my false leg off. I ended up keeping the limb inside the suit so I could put the whole thing on in one go. I'd brought spare parts with me, of course, and a spare leg, but it was a struggle to keep everything in good working order.

In addition to the handicaps of the crew, the boat suffered an additional problem when we were a couple of thousand miles out of Sydney. We had a fax system that supplied us with updates on the weather, and this packed up. It meant our skipper James had to navigate without the benefit of knowing what the prevailing conditions were. Amazingly, though, we moved up the fleet from twelfth place to seventh – quite an accomplishment given everything we had to deal with.

As we approached Cape Town the conditions changed. The storms abated somewhat, and a bright easterly wind picked up – perfect sailing conditions that allowed us to scream towards our destination. Then, when we were just a few miles out of Cape Town, the wind fell and we were becalmed. It was unbelievably frustrating, having navigated such a treacherous ocean, to be so close to our destination and not have sufficient wind to sail the boat. We could see Table Mountain on the horizon, but there was nothing we could do to get any closer to it, so we just opened a couple of bottles of champagne from our stores and sat drinking it on deck while I played my CD of Monty Python's 'Always Look on the Bright Side of Life'. It was, after all, something we'd all learned to do.

We eventually made it into harbour at midnight on 12 April after more than five weeks at sea and ahead of four other boats in the fleet. We felt triumphant at our achievements and pleased to put our feet on solid ground. I had no idea that my life was about to be turned upside down.

My marriage to Sheila wasn't perfect. Whose marriage is? Like all couples, we'd had our ups and downs, and I've no doubt that I contributed as much to the downs as anybody. But we had a beautiful family and plenty to feel blessed about, and I sincerely believed that any problems we'd had had been mended. We'd moved on from those issues, I thought, for the sake of the kids if not for ourselves.

We hadn't been able to afford to fly the whole family over to Cape Town to see me when I arrived, but Sheila had made the journey and after the long, hard weeks of being on board I was looking forward to seeing her. We'd arranged a room in a nice hotel, and the plan was for us to have a good holiday before I set out on the penultimate leg, which would take us from Cape Town to Boston.

Things didn't turn out like that. When Sheila came to Cape Town, she arrived with bad news. My absence, far from making our relationship stronger as I'd hoped it would do, had had the opposite effect. I guess she'd come to the realization that there was more to life than me. She'd met someone else and had come to tell me that our marriage was over.

I was absolutely devastated. I suppose I knew, deep down, that my going away would either make or break our relationship, but I was sure that it would make it rather than break it. It seemed so surreal, to be there in a luxurious hotel in such an amazing part of the world and, rather than being able to enjoy it, to be spending all my time trying to make things right between my wife and myself. I sat in that hotel with her for days on end, talking and talking. Trying, in all honesty, to win her back.

But I couldn't. Sheila had made her decision and I had to accept it. The time came for her to go back, and I was left alone in Cape Town with an empty feeling inside. I didn't blame Sheila for leaving me. Indeed, now I can see that in many ways she did us both a favour by ending things promptly rather than allowing them to drag on.

Moreover, I knew that I'd had a part to play in the break-up of our marriage. I can't pretend, though, that this wasn't a difficult time for me, stuck halfway around the world from my family. So, two days later, I booked a flight back to England. I tried yet again to make amends, but never got anywhere with it.

Returning to South Africa was, for me, one of the greatest challenges of my life. My disability, I could deal with; the rigours of the oceans were not a problem; but saying goodbye to my family when our lives had just changed beyond recognition was one of the most difficult things I'd ever done. I almost didn't return, but in the final analysis I felt I had a duty to all those people who had sponsored me, and to everyone else on the boat. *Time and Tide* had suffered from such a high turnover of crew members that I decided the decision wasn't really mine to make. I couldn't let the others down, and so I flew back to Cape Town with a heavy heart, but a renewed determination to make the most of the rest of the race.

Reunited with my team-mates, I could tell that many of them were worried for me. They had good reason, but in truth I had allowed myself to accept what had happened; to bury the shock and the upset with my determination to complete the race; to accept that it would have been a far worse thing for Sheila and me to have gritted our teeth in a relationship where we weren't happy. It's true that I probably had my quiet moments, thinking about the past and wondering about the future; it's true that perhaps I wasn't as bubbly and boisterous as I had been up to that point. But I was a bit surprised to learn later that the others in the crew had put me on suicide watch. Good to know that they were looking out for me, but a bit of an over-reaction!

Despite this setback, I determined to enjoy the rest of our stopover in Cape Town before embarking on the next leg of the voyage. It was such an amazing place. Africa felt different, and smelled different, from anywhere else I'd ever been. We visited the Table Mountain National Park and saw the African penguins that live on Boulders Beach. When we were moored in Victoria Docks, a man I didn't recognize turned up asking for me. It transpired he was ex-Parachute Regiment and he'd read about *Time and Tide* in the regiment's magazine, *Pegasus*. He invited me to attend an airborne forces weekend in Cape Town. I asked if I could bring some of the crew with me, and so it was that a few of us rocked up at this regimental event. It was the tradition for some of the serving airborne guys to turn up with a Dakota plane and allow the veterans to do a jump. They invited me to go along, but I had to decline as they were jumping with round parachutes and now more than ever I didn't want to risk a heavy landing that would put me out of action for the rest of the race. During the weekend, however, we met an enthusiastic freefall jumper who invited us up to a local parachute centre, so three or four of us went along.

The parachute centre was a few hours' drive from Cape Town, in a place called Citrus Valley. Getting there was not without its risks – we hadn't gone far when we noticed that almost everyone was carrying a side arm, and it wasn't uncommon to see people carrying pistols on holsters round their ankles. We heeded the advice we were given to not stop at traffic lights if there were a lot of kids hanging around. Citrus Valley itself was well named. I remember driving over the brow of a hill and looking down into a vast valley covered with orange and lemon trees, with a small town, a processing plant and a runway cut into them. Once we arrived at the centre I was loaned a parachute, but as I approached the waiting plane wearing my false leg, I got a few strange looks from some of the other skydivers.

'You done many jumps before?' they asked me.

I shrugged. 'One or two,' I said.

They looked a bit suspicious, but we jumped together anyway and in the end I was the only person who managed to hit the landing zone accurately. It was great to be able to add another location to my skydiving portfolio, but it wasn't long before I had to turn my mind back to the more pressing matter of the next leg of the race: Cape Town to Boston. When that was done, we'd be almost home.

When you spend so much time at sea, you get used to seeing nothing but the water. After a while you start to understand the excitement mariners of old must have felt when they spotted land from the top of the crow's nest. For me there's nothing more beautiful than the sight of the land from the sea, and it's a sight you grow to miss. It's impossible to overstate the thrill of approaching new places after a long voyage. Rio was amazing from the sea; Sydney Harbour too. But of all the places we journeyed to during those ten months, none was so spectacular from the ocean as Cape Town.

Table Mountain dominates that part of South Africa. Three and a half thousand feet above sea level, the plateau is two miles wide and visible from huge distances all around. On leaving Cape Town – our fleet having been blessed before its departure by Archbishop Desmond Tutu – we saw the lower land around Table Mountain drop away, until all that was left was the top of the plateau, proud against the horizon. As we sailed away, we were lucky enough to witness a fascinating phenomenon. The 'tablecloth' is a cloud that sits on the top of the plateau and hangs over the edges. A spectacular sight, and one I found it difficult to take my eyes away from as it disappeared over the horizon, leaving us surrounded once more by nothing except the seemingly infinite blue ocean. It was one of those moments when, despite the personal traumas I'd undergone in Cape Town, I was able to remind myself how privileged I was to be part of this remarkable trip.

As had become the norm, we'd had another changeover of crew in Cape Town. Clive and Steve left us. We were rejoined by Stuart Boreham – such an integral member of the whole *Time and Tide* endeavour, who had not been allowed to sail the two Southern Ocean legs – and by

Brendan, whose knee was far from perfect but good enough, he hoped, to continue sailing. There were two newcomers as well: John Spence, who had lost his leg below the knee while he was still a child when he was knocked off his bike by a lorry; and Greg Hammond, who had been born with no lower right arm.

It was 7,000 miles from Cape Town to Boston, and we would be crossing the equator once more, which meant changes in weather patterns as we headed from cold to hot. In racing terms, we didn't do well, and found ourselves trailing the rest of the fleet for most of the leg. In sailing terms, though, much of this leg was spectacular. The winds were good, the seas calm, and the skies clear. We saw beautiful sunsets and magnificent night skies. One night – it was beautifully clear, with the jewelled, inky sky stretching down to the horizon – when we were nearing the eastern seaboard of the United States I saw what looked like a flare in the distance, or a firework. My immediate thought was that a nearby boat was in distress. Unlike a distress flare, however, this light didn't fade away, but kept rising up and up into the heavens. There were two of us on deck. If it had been just me, I'd have dismissed it. After all, the sky was filled with shooting stars, so I'd probably have assumed it was some such astronomical phenomenon. But as we'd both seen it, and both been astonished by its brightness and longevity, we knew it must have been something else. It was only when we got to Boston that we found out what it was we'd seen that night: the Space Shuttle, being launched from Cape Canaveral.

We saw hundreds of flying fish during this leg. They would leap out of the water and sometimes glide across the deck. These kamikaze fish could be a bit of a hazard at times, especially at night – an unseen slippery fish on deck can be the nautical equivalent of a banana skin. One of our crew was hit on the side of the head and nearly knocked out. Enormous Portuguese man-of-war jellyfish floated on the surface. Schools of dolphins and porpoises would leap from the foam, and sometimes they would race with the boat – it was an amazing experience to be out in the dolphins' own environment, a privilege to feel like part of their world. At night they would flash toward the boat, like torpedoes of the natural world, creating moon-lit ripples as they arrived. Now and then a bird would land on the boat out of nowhere, rest its wings for a while, and then continue its journey. You couldn't help wondering where they'd come from, or where they were going to.

There were whales too. Sometimes they would simply be dotted around like floating boulders, but occasionally they would put on a show for us. To see a humpback whale emerge from the water and perform a backflip just 100 metres away was, for me, one of the high points of the entire race.

We had to deal with the doldrums again, however. After the excitement of the Southern Ocean, where a lack of wind is something you can only dream of, this was even more exasperating than it had been the first time round. *Time and Tide* fell so far behind the leading vessel

that it became clear we had no chance of doing particularly well in the race overall, which led to long periods of
frustration and, if I'm honest, boredom. We passed the
time by playing board games on deck, and indulging in
the occasional moment of silliness, such as when the
amputees on board sat for a photo shoot with all their
spare limbs spread out in front of them.

Our arrival in Boston was slow, and we came in last.
Nevertheless, there was a celebratory mood as we made
land – much champagne and press attention, with helicopters hovering and journalists waiting to interview us. Our
accommodation was in the halls of residence at the
Massachusetts Institute of Technology, overlooking the
Charles River. Each stopover had a big prize-giving party,
and this one was held in the city's aquarium. But better
than the parties was Brendan, Grahme and I receiving
word that a prosthetic company in nearby Salem had
invited us to visit them. It would prove to be a significant
trip for me, because they offered to make me a new leg.
This was a life-changing moment.

Up until that point I had been using variations on the
original false leg I'd been given in hospital. This new leg,
which at the time was unavailable through the NHS, was
a different animal altogether. It had a leaf spring and
shock absorber; the carbon foot was designed to shift the
weight of my body as I took a step, using the energy
created by putting my foot down to help me take a step
forward. Compared with what I'd been using previously
– essentially a pole with a block of wood at the end – it

was a revelation. At first it was like standing on a mattress – I would put weight on my new leg and feel like I was sinking into the floor. But I soon got used to it, and knew I could never look back. The new leg was much better for my stump, because it didn't jar it so much and was infinitely more comfortable. Such prosthetics are commonplace for amputees nowadays. Back then I was one of the first people to have use of one, and it's impossible to overstate how much it has improved my life. It meant my stump didn't break down so much, and by extension my hip and my back were in much less pain. And being state-of-the-art, it was ideal for amputees who wanted to remain active. I had no doubt in my mind that this was what I wanted to do.

We had almost completed our circumnavigation of the earth. We'd travelled 27,000 miles and survived some of the most treacherous conditions the sea could throw at us. The final leg, from Boston back to Southampton, felt like little more than crossing the English Channel. For most of us that was a good thing. We'd done so much and been away from home for a long time, and couldn't wait to get back. Some of the crew would finish the race and never sail again; others would turn their back on their old life and aim to spend most of the rest of their lives at sea. But for now we all just wanted to get home.

For me the arrival back in Southampton was bittersweet. I was proud of my achievement, proud that I'd done what I set out to do despite the state of my legs and the hurdles – both physical and psychological – that I'd encountered along the way. It had taken an all-disabled crew 176 days and 18 hours to enter the record books and sail round the world, and the sense of achievement was not lost on any of us. Now, though, we were home, and I was more excited than I could say to see the children again and for them to know that their daddy was back for good. But as I saw the kids waiting in Southampton, along with Sheila and my mum, I knew that my arrival back in the UK did not signal a return to my old way of life. It signalled a transition to a new one, living by myself while I did what I could to continue being a good father after my extended absence.

Some people might think that this was too high a price to pay for my year of living dangerously. I think differently. The race didn't cause my break-up with Sheila, it just accelerated it; and I would like to hope that it gave the children a measure of inspiration to see me pursue a dream, and to be involved with it, despite everything.

And as I acclimatized once more to living on solid ground, rather than on the constant rolling sway of the sea, it gradually became clear to me that the BT Global Challenge was so much more than a race. It had been a life-altering year – a year in which everyone on the boat grew and learned and changed. I'd been away from home for a long time and seen different peoples and places; there had been highs and lows, and physical hardships. In that respect, it was not unlike my military training, and it had a similarly profound effect on me as a person. By pushing myself to my extremes, I'd learned more about myself; by putting myself through the challenge of circumnavigating the globe, I'd grown to understand more about what I was capable of. But it wasn't just about me. *Time and Tide*'s successful voyage was a personal triumph for everyone involved, but, more importantly, I hope that as a crew we achieved something even greater: encouraged the public to think of people like us not in terms of our disability, but in terms of our ability. If we managed to do that, it was worth every ounce of hardship that we experienced along the way.

Chapter Fourteen

Not Forgotten

I moved from the family home to my own place near Aldershot. Back to the real world.

Sheila and I organized a big thank-you party at a lovely hotel on the banks of the Avon in Salisbury, and it turned out to be a beautiful sunny day. We invited everyone who had helped make the trip possible, along with family and friends. It was a way of closing a chapter of my life. Being on my own after that took a great deal of adjustment, however, and there were times when it got me down. I had, after all, lived so closely with the crew of *Time and Tide* for ten months, and I had my new family situation to get used to. But it's not in my nature to be downcast for long. I felt that I'd been given a massive opportunity in taking part in the Global Challenge, an opportunity that was only possible through the generosity of so many people. I wanted to use that in a positive way, to make the best of it.

Some of the crew members of *Time and Tide* and the other competing yachts went off and made a living giving inspirational talks about their experiences. I wasn't that way inclined. I did a few talks to groups on a voluntary basis, but I didn't feel entirely at my ease talking out loud about my experiences. There's a quiet satisfaction to be had when someone realizes you've done something out of the ordinary, but I never felt comfortable announcing the fact to all and sundry. Not being very good at blowing my own trumpet, I would have to find other ways of putting my experiences to good use.

Having sailed round the world, it seemed odd that I didn't have any sailing qualifications to speak of. It's a strange fact that the more complex sailing techniques are not practised on round-the-world voyages, but closer to shore, where tides and wind patterns are more variable. In the middle of the ocean you don't have to worry about how deep the sea is; around coastal areas, hitting the bottom is one of the biggest worries you have. So I decided to put my wealth of experience to good use and obtain my sailing qualifications, working from the bottom up just as I had when I was learning how to skydive. I did this through a charity called the Gwennili Trust, which exists to give disabled people from all walks of life the opportunity to go yachting. It felt fantastic to be in charge of a boat, to be able to make all the small decisions that are necessary to sail successfully. And once I was able to skipper a boat by myself, and with the freedom of not having to work, it meant I could start putting my skills to good use.

Blesma, the charity through whom I had first gone sailing during Cowes Week, was responsible for introducing me to sailing. It seemed only right that I should give something back, both to them and to the Gwennili Trust, by whom I was invited to become a trustee as I was their first member to qualify as a yachtmaster. As a trustee I found myself alongside a brigadier from the special forces and a captain from the Royal Navy; for Corporal Burns to find himself in such company was a real honour.

As I became more involved with Blesma, I started taking the charity's members out on sailing boats, as I still do. We charter either a catamaran or a monohull yacht that has been specially adapted so that a person in a wheelchair can not only get on board, but also move around the deck and sail the boat. There is even a little lift so that they can get below deck. It means we can take somebody out for a sail even when they have the most limited use of their limbs and need 24-hour care. It's amazing how stimulating people find it – so much so that it's often enough for them just to be on deck, let alone raise the sail or get the boat moving.

I returned to Cowes Week with disabled crews; I took part in the Round the Island Race, as well as lots of other races, regattas and cruises, with able-bodied crews as well as ex-Army amputees who wanted, for whatever reason, to get out on a boat. Before this time a group of able-bodied skippers had kindly been volunteering to take disabled crew members out on the water. It was a thrill for me, though, to be able to take guys out by myself, and I hope that it was, in some measure, empowering for them to see what could be done with the application of a little self-belief. The crew and I would be in the same boat in more ways than one, and I think that could only be inspirational for them and me.

Over the next ten years I did literally hundreds of cruises with disabled crews. More amputees and other disabled people than I can count got to experience the wild exhilaration of sailing, and to feel the unbeatable sense of achievement that goes with it. I honestly believe it made their lives richer. But, as is my habit, I wanted to push things a bit further, so in August 2001, a limbless sailing friend Ian Whitting and I set about putting an all limbless crew into the notorious Fastnet Race – the course renowned for its treacherous conditions and on which, in 1979, fifteen people had lost their lives. This was the first time an all-disabled crew had entered the race. It was a great success, and brought a new member into Blesma sailing. Colin Rouse had lost one leg and nearly lost the other when his yacht exploded due to a gas leak. He was a yachtmaster examiner working for the Joint Services Sailing Centre, so brought with him a wealth of experience. We continued with more adventurous sails: the ARC Atlantic Race, the Ondeck Atlantic Challenge, the Caribbean 600. We now even have wounded American servicemen on our trips. I also took part in the 2004 Fastnet Race with an able-bodied crew, and did the Admiral's Cup with a half-disabled and half-professional crew, which represented a steep learning curve for all of us.

In addition to Blesma and the Gwennili Trust, I became involved in another organization, the Not Forgotten Association. This charity came into being in 1919, just after the horrors of the First World War, when a famous singer of the day called Marta Cunningham visited her local hospital and asked if they had any wounded ex-servicemen in their care. She was so appalled at the reply, 'Six hundred', that she started the Not Forgotten Association with the intention of providing entertainment for those disabled ex-servicemen who had made it back from the war. Today it remains a relatively unknown organization, but it still performs an important job, laying on days out for men and women who might otherwise not easily be able to get out and about. They take ex-servicemen to Wimbledon and Ascot, or on canal-boat trips. They also organize battlefield tours. I joined a group of veterans who visited the beaches of the Normandy landings. It was a humbling experience to see these people returning to the place that had so many memories for them, and it choked me up as they surveyed the endless graveyards containing memorials to their fallen friends. An emotional week, but so important to the veterans.

Each year the Not Forgotten Association organizes a garden party at Buckingham Palace which is attended by royalty, and a Christmas party at Clarence House. These events are attended by around 3,000 disabled servicemen, including groups from Headley Court, Blesma, Combat Stress, St Dunstan's, the Chelsea Pensioners, and many more. At a recent garden party the Not Forgotten

Association invited me to greet the Princess Royal, to give a little speech and present flowers on the charity's behalf. I chatted with her afterwards, and explained how I had received my injuries at Warrenpoint and my involvement with disabled sailing. I then went off to join the people from Blesma. Minutes later Princess Anne was presented to this group, and when she caught sight of me her eyes narrowed. 'I've met you before, haven't I?' she said with a smile.

The next time I met her was at the Christmas party at Clarence House. As she talked to our table, escorted by a rather strait-laced brigadier, I once again talked about Warrenpoint and sailing. I wondered if I could brighten her day and make her smile, so at the end of our chat I asked her if she wanted to pull my Christmas cracker. The brigadier wasn't amused. 'The Princess Royal does *not* want to pull your Christmas cracker!' he announced, before escorting her swiftly to the next table of guests. But Princess Anne had a big smile and a twinkle in her eye. She clearly has a great sense of humour. She takes a keen interest in the achievements of the disabled sailors who take to the water through the agency of the various organizations that I'm involved with.

The Christmas parties at Clarence House are also well attended by lots of celebrities who make an effort to lend their support to these charities – people as varied as Tony Blackburn, Vera Lynn, Boney M, the Stylistics, among many others. It's amazing how many different types of people are moved to be involved. It means a lot to so many of the guys that individuals such as Princess Anne and other royals and people in the public eye should take time out to be present at these gatherings. It's easy for them to feel that their costly service to the country has been forgotten; the attention of the royal family makes them realize it hasn't.

My experience in the sailing world opened my eyes to the many other adventurous sporting opportunities that are available to people with disabilities. Having seen what a positive experience the members of Blesma were having on a boat, I became increasingly keen to encourage amputees to spread their wings in all sorts of other ways. With the Not Forgotten Association, I have kayaked the River Spey with a bunch of disabled ex-service guys. It's hard work – seventy-two miles down the river – but a great success and an event which we repeated for three years running.

Then in 1998 I was invited to go on Blesma's annual ski-bob trip. Even I was a little bit perplexed as to how I would manage on the slopes wearing a prosthetic leg, standing on skis, and walking up and down slippery stuff! I'd have loved to go skiing before I lost my leg, but afterwards I never imagined until now that I would manage it. Through Blesma, however, I learned about ski-bikes. These look like ordinary mountain bikes, but the wheels have been removed and replaced with skis. The bikes have a very low centre of gravity, which makes them very easy to ride and practically impossible to fall off. You wear short skis on your legs, but since you're sitting on the bike, it means a leg amputee doesn't have to put any pressure on their stump, which means no pain. It's like off-road mountain biking with skis on, and it's immense fun – so much so that many able-bodied people go ski-biking in preference to regular skiing. They're not a disabled aid – they've been used for over a century on the slopes, and ski-biking has its own sporting body and world championships.

The first time I went to Sölden in Austria, I was absolutely blown away. It didn't matter that because my 'good' foot is so distorted I had to wear a ski boot that was two sizes too big, all padded out to protect the foot, or that I had to stop every twenty minutes to get the blood flowing in the limb once again. I was skiing, and to have the mobility to whizz around for miles and zoom downhill at great speed without the use of an engine gave me the most amazing sense of freedom, one that I never thought I would have. I was able to take part in many ski disciplines, including slaloms and downhill runs, just like able-bodied skiers. By the end of my first trip I was already signing up to go again the following year. I was hooked.

Ski-biking is a particularly popular activity with Blesma, and there are only a limited number of places to go each year. So to maximize my chances of being involved, I decided to work towards my instructor's rating. I went to Austria off my own bat for an instructor's course and learned how to teach the skills of ski-biking, and ever since then I've been going each year to teach amputees who are new to the sport how to do it. It's an extremely rewarding and enriching experience to be able to explain to amputees who think they'll never be able to go skiing that if I can do it they can. I derive as much fun from being part of the organization as from taking part in the actual sport.

The sailing and skiing trips in which I take part with Blesma are more than just holidays. For the limbless ex-servicemen, they are a lifeline. It's no secret that soldiers often find it difficult readjusting to civilian life after many years in the armed forces. But for those who have lost a limb, it's much more difficult. If they don't have the chance to mix with other people who have had the same experiences as them, who understand the issues and difficulties involved in living with such injuries, life can become lonely. These sporting trips give military amputees the chance to relax and enjoy themselves, certainly; but they also allow them to feel part of a group. If you live in a world where, inevitably, you're different from everyone else and you find it difficult to come into contact with other amputees, that's a very important thing. These trips act as therapy. You see guys coming along for a week away and they're often very introverted to start with. Either that or they appear angry or frustrated. They don't feel inclined to give anything a go. I can't do it, it's stupid even to try, is what they are feeling.

But at the end of the week they've seen what they can achieve; more importantly, they've spent a few evenings in the bar with other people who understand their introversion, their anger and their frustration. And even if they've just spent a few hours chatting about amputee issues that most people would never think of, things they might be embarrassed to discuss with other people such as where to buy shoes, they change. You can see the difference it makes to them just being with other people who understand these issues. So often they go home a different person. It feels amazing to be a part of that experience and to help it happen. Those little trips to Austria, or sailing round the Solent or across the Atlantic, have changed countless lives.

Blesma knows how rewarding these experiences can be, so we're constantly looking for new activities to offer our members, in the hope that an increasing number of them will feel that they want to join us. We have older members, for example, who might well think that entering the Fastnet Race is not quite for them. For the past few years Blesma has run an activity week and a golden oldies week, where we offer a bigger range of different pastimes to appeal to a broader spectrum of individuals. The charity has two residential nursing homes, one in Blackpool and one in Crieff in Scotland, fully equipped with all the facilities an amputee might require. Our activity week is based at the Crieff home, and there are all manner of outdoor activities nearby. There's white-water rafting; there are gliders that have been specially modified so that they can be flown by double leg amputees; there's river-bugging, where you're strapped into a kind of inflatable armchair and sent speeding down the rapids; and there's horse riding.

I'd done a little bit of riding in the past, so when I was given the opportunity to get back on a horse during the Blesma activity week, I jumped at the chance. It wasn't quite what I expected. We were hosted by a disabled riding centre where my group included amputees and some paraplegics in wheelchairs. I couldn't wear my false leg at the time, as the stump had broken down, but I didn't think that would be a huge impediment to horse riding. The centre had brought all their volunteers in, so there must have been three or four of them for every one of us. For those of us who couldn't physically get into the saddle there was a horse and trap; the rest of us were only allowed to get on the horse with one person leading and another person following behind. It was as safe and secure as I suppose they felt it had to be – but it wasn't exactly the excitement-packed activity I'd been expecting, and I wasn't having much fun stuck there like a lemon while the horse walked sedately up and down.

I politely turned to one of the instructors. 'Can I take the reins myself?' I asked.

They shook their heads. 'No, no … that's against the rules.'

That was the wrong thing to say to me. I turned round in the saddle so I was facing the wrong way and I beck-oned – a bit grumpily, I suspect – to the owner of the school who was standing nearby. She could see that I wasn't particularly satisfied with the experience. 'All right,' she told me. 'You can do some vaulting.'

'What's vaulting?' I asked.

'Wait and see.'

We returned to the indoor arena, where I got my first taste of horse vaulting. It's like gymnastics on horseback, and I was given a quick demonstration by a teenage girl. She removed the saddle from my horse, replaced it with a pad, and put the horse on a lunge rein. Then she displayed her skills. She ran beside the horse, which circled around the arena, jumping onto its back, and off the other side; she stood on horseback with her arms up in the air; she did handstands. It was amazing to watch.

Once she'd finished, it was my turn.

I learned how to sit sideways on the horse while trotting, and how to lie on my front like Superman. Since I didn't have my false leg I couldn't stand up, but I managed to get up on my knees with my arms out. Then I had to do all this facing backwards – really disorientating and a lot more difficult than the other way round because if you start to lose your balance you can't grab hold of the horse's neck. Typically, I couldn't quite resist trying a handstand – a strange experience as you're being shaken up and down with the movement of the horse, but a lot of fun. And once all the others had seen me do that, they all wanted a go. Even Rob, an arm amputee, managed to do a handstand with one arm. Disabled? Hardly.

Through the Not Forgotten Association, I have come into contact with guys whose injuries may not at first seem to be as bad as those of an amputee, but who have been affected by the brutality of conflict in very profound ways. Suffering through war, I have learned, is not limited

to the physical. In 2006, 3 Para returned from Afghanistan after some of the fiercest fighting of the conflict.
Their bravery under fire during that tour of duty has
become almost legendary, but it came at a cost. Several
guys lost limbs, two of whom subsequently came to join
me at the Airkix wind tunnel in Milton Keynes for some
simulated skydiving experience. It's expensive to get
places in the wind tunnel, and time is limited, so I was a
bit miffed to see that four of the amputees' buddies, who
had no signs of physical damage at all, had come along.

I kept quiet, of course, and we all had our time in the
tunnel, then we all went to a restaurant for a meal and
some drinks, before returning to the hotel where we were
staying the night. We sat in the bar talking and by the end
of the evening I started to wonder if the four able-bodied
guys hadn't suffered more than those who'd lost limbs.
They were suffering from combat stress, which was
threatening to cripple their lives just as badly as a physical injury might have done. To this day I find myself on
the verge of tears when I remember the things they told
me. One of them described the moment when he was on
the top of a building in Helmand Province in the middle
of a firefight. One of his friends was hit and he had to
hold in the poor guy's stomach to stop his guts all spilling
out. He subsequently died.

These are things the human brain should not have to
deal with, and when you've suffered experiences like that,
it seems to me that you qualify for whatever help those
who are injured physically receive, because the long-term

effects can be just as debilitating. Two friends of mine both became alcoholics as a result of their experiences in Northern Ireland. One of them – who had done a lot of undercover security work there – died as a result. The other has stopped drinking, but once you're an alcoholic you're an alcoholic for life, and that's a scar of war that will never leave my friend. It's the support that he receives from charities like Combat Stress and the Not Forgotten Association that keeps him going.

It's such crucial work, because the implications of ignoring combat stress are terrible. I know of one ex-serviceman who was visited by the police. They found him in his combats, living in his kitchen with everything set up as if he was still camping in the jungle. He'd become a complete recluse, unable to function properly in civvy street now that he was back from active service. And I've met another guy who used to be in the Royal Navy – built like a brick outhouse and not the sort of bloke you'd want to be on the wrong side of. He visits a centre run by Combat Stress, where he spends much of his time painting. When I visited him he was painting a picture of the Falklands from the sea; looking round his room, I saw that he'd painted the same picture over and over again – each one slightly different, but all of them showing the same scene. It transpired that he had been on HMS *Sheffield*, the Royal Navy destroyer that had been hit by an Argentine Exocet missile and subsequently sank. The trauma of that event had clearly stuck with him, even thirty years later.

For so many people, leaving the Army and disappearing back into normal life can be a difficult and bruising experience, and you never know if or when the psychological traumas are going to manifest themselves. It could be immediate; it could be months or even years later. The worst thing is that people with psychological scars are so easily forgotten, while those of us with physical injuries are more visible. It is just as beneficial, however, for former soldiers suffering from combat stress to take part in activities with other ex-servicemen. So often you see them coming out of themselves simply by having contact with other people who understand a little of what they've been through. I feel a sense of great pride at being able to work with them, and to share some of the good fortune I've had. I hope that when people see me, and others like me who have an obvious physical manifestation of their injuries, they might be encouraged to remember those whose suffering is less evident but no less extreme. That way we can perhaps help change their lives for the better and make them realize that they are, in fact, not forgotten.

Chapter Fifteen

The Silver Screen

In 1979, when my life changed and I was lying with a broken body in a military hospital, there were dark moments when I wondered how, with such severe injuries, I would possibly find things to fill my life. As time progressed I grew to understand that I could have a positive role, that I could fit my injury around my life rather than my life around my injury. I had been the first one-legged skydiver. I had been part of the first disabled crew to circumnavigate the globe. I had skippered the first disabled crew to take part in the Caribbean 600 yacht race. I felt I was collecting firsts like nobody's business. But it wasn't the firsts themselves that were important. The significant factor was that my achievements were being realized not despite my injury, but *because* of it. If I hadn't been blown up in Northern Ireland and lost my leg, I'd have been – for want of a better phrase – an ordinary person. I was living proof that disabilities needn't be disadvantages. If you approach them in the right way, and with the right frame of mind, they can be quite the opposite. Yet I am, even after all these years, still sometimes surprised by the wealth of opportunities that present themselves.

Although there are not that many jobs for amputees, they do pop up now and again. In 1999 someone at Blesma took an enquiry. The director Ridley Scott was making a new film. It starred Russell Crowe, Oliver Reed and Joaquin Phoenix, and it was to be filmed in Malta and the UK. The film, of course, was *Gladiator*, and they needed some amputees to appear on screen during the gory battle scenes. The call came through to me. Was I interested in taking part? You bet I was.

This was something I would never have even thought about getting into; something that, if I hadn't been injured, would simply have been outside of my sphere of imagination. I was so excited by the whole prospect. There were nearly 800 extras on set when I turned up, of which about twenty were arm or leg amputees. It was March when we filmed, not far from where I live near Aldershot, but the snow was going sideways. It was freezing, but that didn't matter to us – we had costume armour and rabbit skins to keep us warm! There appeared to me to be no expense spared on this massive logistical exercise, and I was so impressed by how such a mammoth shoot could be run so smoothly – it rather appealed to the organized, military side of me.

Most of the scenes in which I took part were just in the background, but there was one in which I had a little more to do. The director told me to lie on a bed in a big tented hospital, and my stump was made up to look all bloodied and ragged – as if it had just been hacked off with an axe. I was to lie there while Russell Crowe walked past and delivered a few encouraging words to his wounded soldier. I wasn't given much more in the way of direction, but I didn't think I could just lie there and do nothing, so once the camera was rolling I clutched my stump and started writhing in agony. The actors who played medics responded immediately, pinning me down and mopping my brow as I groaned and screamed in pain.

Unfortunately my first foray into the world of acting ended up on the cutting-room floor – as you can imagine, I was devastated when I went to the cinema fully expecting to see myself on screen and I wasn't there! But I'd loved the experience and, chatting to some of the other amputees, I learned that there were mainstream actors' agencies who supply limbless actors to the TV and film industry. I couldn't believe I'd been an amputee for so long without realizing this, and I signed up with a couple of agencies immediately.

I now take on a couple of extras roles a year, and in the times since *Gladiator* the roles have added up. I play a mean one-legged beggar – a role that seems to have cropped up several times in several movies. I was a war veteran in *Atonement*; I crashed around on crutches in *Clash of the Titans*; I had parts in *Longitude* and *Elizabeth: The Golden Age*, in which a cannonball took my leg off. I've even been a peg-legged, donkey-riding postman in an

Anthony Trollope adaptation, during which I was part-
nered with a fourteen-hand stud donkey from Weston-
super-Mare. His day job was siring donkeys for the
seaside donkey-riding market. I couldn't help wondering
if he had an even better life than me. When I turned up
for my day's shooting, one of the production team
approached me.

'You'll need a stick,' he said.

'What for?'

He looked over at the donkey. 'That animal's not going
to move just because you ask him nicely,' he said.

I found myself a small stick and went back onto the
set. The production guy shook his head. 'You'll need a
bigger one than that,' he told me. He was right. It was a
stubborn old beast. It took all my strength on the reins
just to turn his head in the right direction, and then
several good whacks from the extended stick before he
deigned to move.

Invariably the production teams on these films are very
health and safety conscious, and they're forever sitting me
down on the edge of things and asking me if I want a
nice cup of tea when in fact I'd much rather be getting
into the thick of things. I'm always asking them to let me
fall down flights of stairs, or fly through the air, but it's
often a battle to persuade them to let me do something a
bit more challenging – even though with my military
background and my time in the Red Devils I have the
ideal background for some low-level stunt work. In order
to give myself opportunities to land some of the more

exciting roles, I went on a combat riding course. We learned how to ride horses in lots of different ways: one-handed and carrying a sword; hands-free, steering the horse by squeezing your legs. The horses – mostly ex-polo ponies that have been trained to cope with all sorts of situations – were amazing animals and seemed perfectly at their ease even when we were learning how to gallop at another rider and cross our wooden swords. At one point I managed to break my sword, but that wasn't nearly so dramatic as the moment my false foot fell off. The instructors looked rather alarmed, and told me I couldn't continue, but I still had the bulk of my false leg and was able to grip the horse firmly, so it wasn't really as debilitating as it looked. And when, later in the day, my horse tripped up and did a forward roll, I was glad the foot had gone; if it had got stuck in the stirrup when the horse rolled, the animal could have come down on top of me.

I have been able to do some work with the stunt teams. In *Band of Brothers* I had a false leg stuffed full of explosives and fake blood, and had to go flying through the air attached to a jerk wire, and it meant a speaking role and work with a dialogue coach. More exciting than playing yet another one-legged beggar, though if that was all I got offered, I'd be more than happy. Film work is not only good fun, it's another way in which I'm able to turn my disability into a positive, another aspect to my life that has come about not despite my injuries, but because of them. It's brilliant for me to be able to get out, do new things, and meet new people, and there are unexpected advantages. On the recent *Robin Hood* movie, where I played a war veteran from the Crusades, I met my new partner, Linda, who was also employed as an extra. That could never have happened if I'd not been blown up all those years ago.

Amputee friends of mine have also managed to have their moments of fame. Take Steve Gill – a big, colourful guy who lost both legs and the use of one eye at the age of 19 in a bomb blast in Belfast. Did it hold him back? Not a bit. He has eight children, is a wheelchair basketball coach, has sailed across the Atlantic, and as I write this he's a contestant in the *Big Brother* house. Steve does a lot within Blesma in terms of talking to recent amputees and showing them that, in his words, losing a limb 'is not the end of the world', and being on a widely watched show like *Big Brother* can only be a positive thing when it comes to raising awareness of the issues amputees face. People like Steve, and my good friend Charlie Streather, who with one leg and other injuries not only takes part in our events but organizes them too and is now employed as a welfare officer with Blesma, do an amazing job of raising the profile of amputees.

In addition to my work as an extra, my experience in parachute rigging has led to some involvement on the stunt preparation side of the industry. I made and fitted a load-carrying harness for Angelina Jolie in *Tomb Raider* – as well as for her eleven stunt doubles. And when a rocket sledge disappears over an ice cliff in the James

Bond movie *Die Another Day*, the parachute that shoots out of the back was one of my creations.

Being on the film sets of these various projects led to me meeting a lot of other amputees who were doing the same thing. We started to talk about setting up our own agency for amputee actors on a not-for-profit basis. That way the guys we put up for jobs could keep all the money they earned rather than pay a percentage of it to a mainstream agency. In March 2004, Amputees in Action was formed, and we've helped a lot of people find work in many different film and TV productions.

Film work is one way in which I can make something positive out of the way I look. But it also led to another very important activity with which I and other amputees have started to involve ourselves.

As I write, British troops have been mostly withdrawn from Iraq, but many are still fighting the Taliban in Afghanistan. It's a brutal and costly war. We hear in the news media of so many deaths that they have become the norm rather than the exception, but what we don't hear so much about are those soldiers who, though not killed in the line of duty, have suffered terrible injuries as a result of the Taliban's tactics. Just like the IRA when I was deployed to Northern Ireland, the enemy in Afghanistan have become expert in the art of constructing improvised explosive devices. Our troops have been given bigger and safer vehicles to deal with this threat, but the bigger the vehicles, the bigger the enemy make the IEDs. And in any case, the situation in that country is such that most of the patrolling needs to be done on foot rather than by vehicle. The net result is a host of servicemen returning from that terrible war as amputees. We hear very little about them, but they are an almost daily reality of life in Afghanistan.

What happens to these amputees once they get home is one issue. Almost as important, though, is the need to give our young soldiers some idea of what they can expect on the battlefield when one of their colleagues is injured by an IED, because without adequate training, there's no doubt that there would be fewer amputees coming home, but more deaths. One of the members of Amputees in Action, Albert Thompson, had lost his leg out in Iraq and knew something of the trauma involved for the guys on the ground when such a thing happens. He saw an opportunity for us to make a difference in this respect, and suggested that we diversify into casualty simulation with the Army, where amputees are brought in to inject some real-life colour into simulated training exercises. This was something that had never been done before, and everyone agreed that it would be a very good idea. Things got in the way, however – not least that most people preferred to be on a movie set than a cold, wet training field in Wiltshire – so now there are two amputee agencies: Amputees in Action and Albert's Amputee Casualty Simulations.

Having real-life amputees for casualty simulation was an entirely new concept. Previous casualty simulation had been a much cruder affair – sometimes as little as a perfectly healthy guy lying on the floor with a sign round his neck saying 'This man has a broken leg', so that the trainee soldiers could make a decision about how best to treat them. Albert's agency allowed the Army to take their pre-deployment exercises to a new level of realism, and Amputees in Action soon started supplying personnel too.

As a result of this, the pre-deployment exercises that British soldiers now undergo before being posted to Afghanistan prepare them much more effectively for the brutal reality of life in the field. We amputees are made up to look as if we have been freshly wounded, as medically accurate as possible, and we're encouraged to scream and act as if we really have just sustained terrible injuries. No matter that this happens in the green countryside of England rather than the arid sands of Afghanistan: it's still not a pretty sight. We've done exercises with everyone from newly recruited privates to special forces; we've trained with live rounds being fired on several different fronts, and helicopter gunships firing overhead.

These exercises are very hard work. They always take place in the middle of the night; it's invariably cold and damp and it always lasts for ages. But if it's hard for us, it's even harder for the soldiers. Real bullets flying overhead, real amputees on the ground, screaming and with blood pumping from their missing limbs as if they have a genuine arterial bleed, thanks to a blood bag secreted in our clothes. The troops are expected to put a tourniquet on the wound to stem the bleeding and hopefully save a life – all this with the explosions of the battlefield going on all around them. And since we know what they're supposed to do and not supposed to do, we can react in a clinically correct fashion by passing out or staying conscious according to the treatment we receive. As a preparation for the theatres of war in which our troops now find themselves, it's pretty accurate. Each scenario we perform is based on something that actually happened in theatre.

The gory reality of what a serious casualty looks like is a great shock for most of the young soldiers that we train. You can tell by the look in their eyes. No matter that it's wet and cold, no matter how tired they are or how little they want to be there, no matter how unenthusiastic they are about the exercise: seeing a real amputee scream-ing in pain and clutching the stump of his severed limb as it pumps blood at you is a jolt, a reality check. And it's an invaluable part of their preparation, because it genuinely does save lives. From the very first time amputees were used in casualty simulation, the reports came back from the troops that it had somewhat desensitized them to the horror of battlefield casualties, allowing them to think with a clear head when the time comes to deal with these situations for real. There is no doubt that there are people alive today, albeit with awful injuries, who would not have survived had it not been for our input. There's a real buzz to be had from knowing you've been involved in that. A feeling of worth.

There's another advantage to having amputees involved with soldiers about to deploy for the first time. For these young men, the fear of losing a limb is very real. Many of them will tell you that they're more scared of that than of losing their life. It's a positive experience for them to spend time with us after the exercises and to see that our lives haven't ended just because we've lost limbs, that we're just ordinary blokes capable of being active and having a laugh. I don't think for a moment it takes the fear away for them, but I do think it helps them put it in some sort of perspective, and hopefully makes their gruelling tours of duty just that little bit easier.

My life now is fuller than I ever thought it could be. Too full, some might say. I have a whole host of things that I intend and want to do, but the time never seems to come around for me to do them. To be truthful, I wouldn't have it any other way. Staying active is my way of dealing with things. I know that if I were to stop and allow myself to dwell for too long on certain aspects of my life, I would risk some very low moments. Not an instant goes by that I don't experience pain in my legs – a dull, constant pain that drains me of energy and sometimes drags my mood down to rock bottom; and the guilt of being a survivor of Warrenpoint is something that will live with me until the day I die. There are mental scars that are too deep to heal, but I know that as long as I refuse to allow my life to be compromised, and as long as I can help others do the same, then the symptoms of those scars can at least be lessened.

For many years I did whatever I could to put the past behind me. Packaged away in a little box in my mind, the memory of Warrenpoint couldn't harm me, and I suppose that in a way I was too scared to unpack it. In recent years, however, I have started to revisit the past. In part, it is so that I can talk to the young soldiers with whom I do casualty simulation about what happened that day, because I know that the more they understand about the realities of war, the better equipped they will be to handle it. But it's also for me, so that I can come to terms with my own past.

Every year there is a memorial service for the victims of the Warrenpoint bombings at the military cemetery in Aldershot. For more than thirty years I stayed away. It wasn't that I didn't want to mark the anniversary of that day, and indeed I always did so in my own way, with a moment of silence and a poignant thought for the memory of those friends of mine who died, or perhaps the raising of a glass. On occasion I would organize a parachute jump for some of the Blesma guys in order to raise money for that charity. But the guilt of being a survivor stayed with me, and I found the thought of being with the families of those who had died unbearable. Warrenpoint was something I'd only ever been able to deal with by putting it behind me. By living my life in as positive a way as possible. By honouring the memory of what happened that day, but not being held back by it. It wasn't until 2009 that I found the courage to go to the annual memorial service.

The cemetery is a beautiful place – remarkably peaceful given that it is the resting place for those who died in often terrible ways. I found being there such a rewarding experience. I saw people that I hadn't seen for many years, and met the families of some of those who had died. And although I felt overwhelmed by the memories, I was also humbled by the fortitude of those families. The effects of Warrenpoint are obvious to anyone who looks at me and sees that I'm an amputee. But those families carry less visible scars, and in many ways they have had to struggle to keep their lives positive every bit as much as I have.

I'm 49 years old. When I look to the future, I know that the pain in my legs, and the damage I've sustained, is likely to get worse, not better. From time to time I've had to go into hospital to have the bone in my stump ground down, because it continues to grow ever so slowly. And there remains the possibility that my 'good' foot will have to be amputated at some stage as it continues to break down and the discomfort I experience increases. I try not to let this worry me. Over the years I have managed to find activities that don't require me to use my legs too much. When you're sailing, you can sit down; the same goes for ski-biking; when you skydive, you have to walk out to the aircraft, but in freefall there's no weight on your legs. I feel confident that I'll continue to do these things well into the future, until my brain becomes more of an issue than my body.

Last year I organized a motorbike ride from Land's End to John O'Groats. Some of our guys were missing arms, had leg amputations above the knee, and one even had both legs missing. How fortunate I am to know these men, and I would never think about reining myself in. These activities are my way of coping. Take them away, and I might not cope any more. And how could I even think about not living my life to the utmost, when I know that so many people who were with me that day in Warrenpoint were unable to live their lives at all, and that my lot could so easily have been theirs?

So even during my low moments – and there have been many – I try to keep my sense of humour, to make people laugh, and ensure that my problems do not become their problems. And when I do get depressed, I'm lucky enough to be able to spot it when it's happening. Depression normally sneaks up on me like a thief when everything's going right and I've got nothing pressing to do. Perhaps that's another reason why I try so hard to keep busy.

On the whole, though, I'm always finding reasons to be cheerful. When I look back over my life, I feel there is much to be proud of. Out of all my achievements, however, nothing makes me quite so proud as my three children. They've all grown up now into lovely, kind people with great partners, and I feel very lucky to have them in my life. As they were growing up I was always very conscious that I didn't want to be the sort of pushy parent who tries to force their kids into doing and liking the same sort of things that they do. Throughout their childhood, Ben,

Georgina and John were surrounded by skydiving. We spent many weekends at parachute centres, and with Dad being in the Red Devils the sport could hardly not be on their radar. But I never encouraged them unduly to take it up. I was mindful of a friend of mine who had his daughter jumping out of planes from the moment she was allowed to. She'd done more than 200 jumps before she confessed to her dad that she didn't really like it! He was mortified, of course, and I certainly didn't want to put myself in that position.

So I never pressured my kids to start skydiving, and indeed Georgina has no interest in it whatsoever. But Ben and John both started jumping at 16 and became qualified in their own right. One of the proudest things I've ever done is skydive individually with my boys and see the smiles on their faces and the buzz they get from it. I don't know how many other people have had the privilege to jump with their sons. Not many, I'm sure, and I feel very special to be one of the few. I'd love to get Georgina in the air too, so that the four of us can fly together. I don't think it's very likely, but a guy has to have some goals, doesn't he?

Even though I've lived with my disability for a long time now, I'm still learning about new ways in which to improve my life. A few months ago I was given a puppy. Like me, Fudge has a leg missing – the only one of a litter of six. How could I resist? Fudge makes do remarkably well with only three legs, and nothing seems to phase her – the sound of airplanes, the sound of motorbikes, even being on a yacht. She's like a doggie version of me. I knew before I adopted her, however, that taking her for a walk would be a problem, so I managed to get myself a power trike – like a wheelchair with a motorized front end. It's changed my life: I used to be the person who sat at the edge of the woods, looking in while everyone enjoyed their walk inside. Now I can join them, and so can Fudge – with the added benefit that if she gets tired, she can sit on my knee. Half of me regrets not having used aids such as this before, but really life is too short for regrets. I'm just looking forward to using the rest of the time I have to its full potential, because I know of so many people who haven't been able to do so.

My story could easily have been so different. If I'd been sitting in another seat in the truck on that day in 1979, I would never have woken up after the blast. When you come close to losing your life, your view of the world changes. Everything else you experience becomes a bonus. An extra. And so, despite all the injuries I sustained, I have never had a sense of being anything other than very, very lucky, and I've never wanted to do anything other than squeeze the very last drop of enjoyment out of my life. When I lay in that hospital bed so many years ago, my body broken and burned, my life hanging by a thread, I never for a moment imagined that I would ever jump out of an airplane again, or set foot on a boat – let alone a 67-foot yacht sailing round the world. I've found, however, that these things *are* possible. They *can* be done. My fervent hope is that, by refusing to be held back by my disability, I can inspire others in the same situation to do the same.

The wars we now face mean that an unprecedented number of single, double and triple amputees are returning to our shores. They face difficult times ahead. I know that better than most. I also know that the story of Warrenpoint isn't just *my* story. It's the story of many soldiers, in the past and in the future, whose names we will never know and whose faces we'll never recognize. If the only thing I ever achieve is to make them realize that their life does not have to stop just because they've lost a limb, I will consider *mine* a life well lived. And while it wouldn't make up for the horror, the carnage and tragedy of the Warrenpoint bombings, it would at least salvage something from the wreckage.

Dedication

This book is dedicated to all those who lost their lives at Warrenpoint, Northern Ireland, on 27 August 1979, and to their families.

ANDREWS, Corporal Nicholas J. (2 Para) – aged 24

BARNES, Private Gary I. (2 Para) – aged 18

BEARD, Warrant Officer Walter (2 Para) – aged 31

BLAIR, Lieutenant Colonel David (Queen's Own Highlanders) – aged 40

BLAIR, Private Donald F. (2 Para) – aged 23

DUNN, Private Raymond (2 Para) – aged 20

ENGLAND, Private Robert N. (2 Para) – aged 23

FURSMAN, Major Peter (2 Para) – aged 35

GILES, Corporal John C. (2 Para) – aged 22

IRELAND, Lance Corporal Chris G. (2 Para) – aged 25

JONES, Private Jeffrey A. (2 Para) – aged 18

JONES, Corporal Leonard (2 Para) – aged 26
JONES, Private Robert D.V. (2 Para) – aged 18
MacLEOD, Lance Corporal Victor (Queen's Own
    Highlanders) – aged 24
ROGERS, Sergeant Ian A. (2 Para) – aged 31
VANCE, Private Thomas R. (2 Para) – aged 23
WOOD, Private Anthony G. (2 Para) – aged 19
WOODS, Private Michael (2 Para) – aged 18

Acknowledgements

I must thank everyone involved with the My Story competition for the opportunity to enter and put my thoughts on paper. Thanks to David Harris for emailing me about the competition, and to Melanie for all your help and encouragement in writing my entry.

Thank you Adam Parfitt for listening and turning my words into print.

The events described in this book are, to the best of my recollection, as they happened. Owing to the constraints of time and space it has not been possible to cover everything I would have liked. Many people should have been mentioned and thanked for helping to shape my life and make it what it is today. I am so sorry it was a secret from you all. I feel it would have been so much fuller and more interesting had I been able to talk to you.

Thank you to Vicky McGeown and all at HarperCollins for your support and patience. You have been wonderful.

And finally, thank you Lynn for helping me see it to the end.